Law-de-da!

Lampooning the laws in our lives

by Geo F Takach

Peppercorn Press

Canadian Cataloguing in Publication Data

Takach, George Francis
Law-de-da! Lampooning the laws in our lives

ISBN 0-919311-27-X

1. Social norms–Humour. 2. Canadian wit and humour (English)* I. Title
PS8589.A42L38 1998 C818'.5402 C98-910911-9
PR9199.3.T345L38 1998

First printing: September 1998

Portions of this volume were published previously in magazines or performed before a live audience. However, any laughter that you may experience is spontaneous, with no electronic enhancements.

This is a work of diction. Any resemblance to living persons is just an eerie coincidence. I mean, there are literally billions of us out there. Any resemblance to deceased persons is truly bizarre, because there are no corpses depicted in these pages.

If you purchased this volume without its cover, then you're missing out. The design is *really* nifty.

Book design & typesetting Bonnie Sadler Takach, *Laff Artz Comedia*

Illustrations
© Bonnie Sadler Takach (pp. 3, 31, 81, 91, 99, 125, 129, 143, 191, 207, 208, 211 & all "Rules" pages)
© Lorne Shapiro (pp. 12 (bottom), 79)
© John Sojak (pp. 1, 9, 19, 25, 45, 71, 83, 127, 201)
© Geo F Takach (pp. 39, 49, 59, 119, 183)

Photo of author in a flap Merle Prosofsky

Excerpt from Robertson Davies' speech from *One Half of Robertson Davies* (Toronto: Macmillan of Canada, 1977) © Robertson Davies, used with the kind permission of Pendragon Ink
Excerpt from *A Funny Thing Happened on the Way to the Boardroom* (New York: John Wiley & Sons, Inc., 1988) © Michael Iapoce
Excerpt from *Reader's Digest (*December 1993) © David Halberstam

Peppercorn Press
Suite 2390, Commerce Place, 10155-102 Street
Edmonton, Alberta, Canada T5J 4G8
phone (403) 424-5345, fax (403) 425-6451*
**After January 25, 1999: phone (780) 424-5345, fax (780) 425-6451*
e-mail: publish@sprint.ca
We welcome your comments.

Printed in Canada by DeJong Printing Ltd.

"I cannot recall a time
when I was not conscious of the
deep, heaving, rolling ocean of hilarity
that lies so very near the surface
of life in most of its aspects."

Robertson Davies, Canadian author,
in a speech to the Cosmos Club of Washington, DC on April 6, 1977

This wave is dedicated to Judit and The Chief,
who not only saw my rolling ocean,
but celebrated it.

Contents

Law-de-da!

Lampooning the laws in our lives

Law-de-da! Lampooning the laws in our lives

Law-de-da! Lampooning the laws in our lives

So many rules, so little rhyme

1

Celebrating the utter absurdity of the law

LAWS, LAWS, LAWS EVERYWHERE. Lurking on endless shelves groaning with musty statute books in libraries. Buried in bursting binders in office supply rooms. Roaring at us from road signs. Swirling around our subconscious and dredged up each time we need to squelch a belch during delicate dental work.

We can hardly breathe without running into, or afoul of, some kind of rule, regulation, code or custom. This wouldn't be so bad if they all made sense. But since the rules that we live by reflect the breadth of human wisdom, passion and experience, they are as loony as we are.

There must be a sound explanation for this. An easy guess would be that our lawmakers are deeply stupid people. But this is a callow crock, or as the French Disney people say, a mighty canard. Our legislators, bureaucrats and trend-setters can't be stupid, because *we* put them there.

The real reason that "the law is a ass" relates to what we expect of it. We want our rules to be as stable as Stonehenge, as predictable as Don Cherry's suits, as durable as the Iceman's butt. But we also want them to be as fluid as Niagara Falls, as flexible as Jim Carrey's face, as timely as an insider stock tip. Thorough, but efficient. All-encompassing, but non-intrusive. Spending like Santa, but saving like Scrooge.

This book celebrates the utter absurdity of it all, and tangoes, rose-in-mouth, with the thorny question of why we should have rules anyway.

Unlike other, possibly better-known volumes, it won't cure you of your bad habits—though it may start you on some new ones. But by revelling in our absurdities, it may help you sneak some well-deserved snickers into your days. Or at least give you the satisfaction of knowing that the rules in your life may not be as crazy as what you will find on these pages.

Enjoy.

Be well.

Take no prisoners.

Geo F Takach

Edmonton Alberta Canada

September 1998

Rules for working on the assembly line

2

Source

Raven Lyrwain Moonglow

Occupation

Druid

Residence

Butt of Lewis, Outer Hebrides, Scotland—
and the cosmos in general

Motto

"The best things in life are tree."

Rules

1 Arrive at work in the proper attire, with the appropriate tools. Be careful not to cut yourself with your scythe, get mistletoe berries on your white robes, or drop your magic cauldron on the shop steward's toe.

2 Report industrial accidents to the gods, and treat all but the most serious cases with dried serpent spittle. In calamitous instances, wave a Bell Branch to ward off malevolent spirits.

3 Reduce your sensitivity to repetitive strain injury by spending your coffee breaks sleeping under the skin of a freshly slaughtered bull. When you wake, it is likely that you will have forgotten all about your sore wrists.

4 Be wary of misunderstandings among the unenlightened. No matter how pure your intentions, it is unwise to refer to your colleagues as "earth-mothers," their lunchboxes as "cabbalistic ritual tools" and their bathroom breaks as "sacred quests for the Grail."

5 Dare to dance to your own harpist. If your co-workers mock you, tell them they can forget about those front-row seats at Stonehenge next June.

6 It is vital to refresh your spirit. When the need arises, lay down your tools, flee to the woods and listen. The voices of the deities echo in the whispering wind, the call of the wren and the clatter of your mailbox receiving your unemployment cheque.

Seeking asylum—
and trying not to end up in one

3

A misfit's adventures in crime and punishment

I HAVE A CONFESSION TO MAKE.

I am a refugee from a cult. A cult of people with glazed eyes, flowing robes, and an obsessive devotion to a higher power. I used to practise law.

There are three reasons why people go into law: (1) the higher power that I just mentioned—money; (2) a deluded desire to save the world; or (3) the inability to find anything better to do. Although I fit in somewhere between reasons (2) and (3), I never did fit in at law school.

In my first year, I wrote musical case briefs and skits to unleash on my unsuspecting classes. (A dredged-up specimen appears on page 125.) I'd answer exam questions in the form of one-act comedies starring two flatulent lawyers who'd argue opposite sides of the case. I'd get my papers back with comments like, "Shakespeare gets an A-plus, you get a C-minus." Although first year law wasn't the best two years of my life, I did come out of it with quite a few plays.

In my second year, I learned the importance of tradition. One zealous bunch of students set the tone for a future wave of disbarments by filching $3000 in photocopying from their own association. By my final year, after reading about the glut of lawyers, it dawned on me that law school couldn't be that tough after all.

When I passed the bar, the distinguished presiding judge welcomed me into an "ancient and honourable" profession. Well, after more than five years of practising law, I felt ancient, and had about all the honour I could stand.

The marble lobbies gave me the shivers. My ties felt like chains. And on really bad days, I was convinced that my dictaphone was the wrong end of Elmer Fudd's hunting rifle. ("*Ooh*, that wascawy wawyer!") But most of all, I couldn't stomach belonging to a profession that would have me as a member. Freedom was calling, echoed by the character-building prospect of poverty. So I quit practising and started doing the real thing.

I wasn't the first refugee in my family. My parents risked their necks to flee the coup when the Soviets had the Hungarian freedom-fighters for breakfast in 1956. I asked my father what communism was like. He puffed on his pipe and said, "Son, it's like this. You put a 'yes' vote in one box, or they put you in the other."

On my first day of school, I found the other kids talking in a strange, new language. That's when I *really* learned something. In their haste to survive in a new world, my parents had forgotten to tell me about English. I mean, here I was in a class of 25, and not a single mention of goulash, paprika or even Stalin.

So I slapped a few of them in the arm and said, "Speak Hungarian like a normal guy." They slapped me back, all hell broke loose, and the teacher had to call in the secret police—who, as it turned out, was actually the principal. I was sure my parents would be proud of me, though. I refused to confess to *anything.*

My teacher, Mrs. Jowett, taught me English. But it came with a rich Scottish brogue, which I finally got rid of after nine months, three weeks and one bowl of haggis.

But I still *looked* different. It was the 1960s. The other kids wore blue jeans, tie-dyed shirts and sparkling new athletic footwear. I wore the haunting browns and greys of Hungarian People's State Garment Collective Number 51.

Today, it seems like a short trip down the rack from those grey hand-me-downs to the grey suits of my practising days. But they had little in common beyond colour. Although English and its sexy cousin, French, fit just fine, the language of the law remains foreign to me, despite spending a decade swimming in it; tailoring two law textbooks; and buttonholing bar admission students while teaching legal writing classes.

We learn a lot of different laws in our lives. But laws and ethics are not always a perfect fit. In my experience, our ethics have less to do with an externally prescribed set of laws than with our own, internal code of behaviour—an evolving code, shaped by our beliefs, our experience and our collective responsibility to leave the world an even better place than we found it.

So if something doesn't suit you, you can do three things. Be a walking monument to misfits, with all of the attendant altercations. Do alterations, and make it fit. Or shred the suit and try another size or style. But if you do, don't spend a lot of time in the changing room. It tends to be cramped, cluttered and away from the real action. Besides, unless you're some kind of model, there's little material gain in standing around half-dressed.

Rules for taking an atheist to mass

Source
Giuseppe "The Face" Fenuzzicello
Occupation
Devoted family man
Residence
Marsala Castelvetrano, Sicily, Italy
Motto
"The Lord is my shepherd, but I am nobody's sheep."

Rules

1 Appeal to the human fascination with ritual, the reverance for tradition and the instinct of self-preservation—if you know what I mean.

2 Stress the fine architectural heritage of the church, and the unique burial opportunities in the crypt.

3 Let them "work off" the service later, with five free bets in the casino downstairs.

4 Tell them at least it's not a funeral service. Not yet, anyway.

5 A great way to make the three hours pass more swiftly: see if they can tell the worshippers from the gargoyles.

6 Offer them a 12-course meal if they make it to the novenas without conscientiously objecting—and a 12-gun salute if they don't.

Opening salute

5

Being a brief introduction to the introduction

AMONG THE FIRST RULES WE LEARN is how to introduce ourselves. Introductions are a telling reflection of the human condition. Much can be gleaned from how we introduce anything, be it ourselves, our long-lost half-brother, Oswald, or touchy subjects like what we did to the car last night.

The origins of introductions are hotly debated in academic circles, and coldly debated in the Arctic and Antarctic Circles. According to revisionist creationist theory, the phenomenon began in the Garden of Eden with the immortal words, "Madam, I'm Adam"—also history's first recorded palindrome and minimalist poem rolled into one.

On the other hand (or foot, depending on whether *Homo erectus* is evolved), Darwinist orthodoxy holds that the introduction started with our cave-dwelling forebears. They would stumble over each other while foraging for elderberry roots and other gastronomic delights of the Stone Age. These chance encounters blossomed from grunts and high-pitched wails into more refined repartee, as humans developed the ability to walk on two legs (early efforts being called the "preamble") and conduct themselves appropriately at formal state dinners.

In any case, the introduction was well served when humans came up with language and began to identify each other. A leading theory holds that people were initially named for their physical characteristics. This would explain monikers like "The Fair One," "The Stout One" and "The Malodorous One."

As folks became more civilized, they would introduce themselves with more diverse names, such as Tabitha (Aramaic for "gazelle"), Edgar (Old English for "successful spearman") and Moon Unit (hippie American for "Tabitha" or "Edgar"). By the 11th century, the populace had outgrown its ability to come up with new names. Not blind to this, the Venetians dusted off the old Roman custom of using surnames to designate clans or tribes. These would derive from the names, attributes, habits or occupations of family members. Thus, Norbert, the son of Alma, came to introduce himself as Norbert Almason; a light-haired Spaniard became Blanco ("White"); and a French teetotaller became Boileau ("Drinkwater").

Eventually, people divined customs that made introducing each other less odious, if not outright pleasant. But these new rules had a strong practical purpose, too. When two passersby offered each other a right hand to clasp, it was not only a gesture of friendship or courtesy, but a convenient check for concealed weapons. The scheme was not foolproof, though. It never worked against lefties.

The first known guide to proper introductions and courteous behaviour in general was chiseled out by Ptah-hetep, a senior bureaucrat in Egypt in about 2400 BC. His monograph, *The Instructions of Ptah-hetep,* led polite folk to refer to social misfits as "hoisted by their own Ptah" or "out of hetep with the times."

History abounds with great introductions. In about 350 BC, Plato's nephew, Speusippus, gave us the earliest surviving codified introduction to natural history, mathematics and philosophy—a forerunner of the encyclopedia, but probably not sold door to door. (To his credit, he summed up Pythagoras' hypotheses squarely, rather than taking sides.) In the 15th century, the printing pioneer, Johannes Gutenberg, stressed the need to make a good first impression. And the noteworthy Romantic pianist, Frédéric Chopin, keyed into the prelude as a form of art, although it didn't catch the public's ear until people figured out that it was a piece in its own right, rather than an introduction to a larger work.

The grandest introduction of all must be the well-known exchange between Dr. David Livingstone, a British explorer and missionary who had set off for the African jungle and failed to return for high tea, and Sir Henry Morton Stanley, a journalist and explorer dispatched by an American newssheet to find him in 1871. Sir Henry's legendary greeting—"Dr. Livingstone, I presume"—is a paragon of dry wit and fluid elegance.

Inspired by these and other precedents, the art of the introduction and the rules that go with it continue to thrive. Canada's contribution—the effusive "How's it goin', eh?"—and cheeky American entries like "What are *you* looking at?" and "This is a stick-up!" are already social classics.

So the introduction is an invaluable and inviolable institution, evolving with us through the ages. Although some may conclude, at least initially, that the introduction needs no explanation (least of all an introduction), it is always best to be forward-looking and to preface facts. After all, even the most final conclusion can get ahead with a good introduction.

Rules for meeting hostile beings from outer space

Source

Herschel B. Potts

Occupation

Retired TV repairman

Residence

Yazoo City, Mississippi, USA

Motto

"If it ain't broke, call me anyway. Emmy and I could always use the money."

Rules

1 Tuck in your shirt and wear a hat. They'll respect you more if you dress good.

2 Take the cat along. I read someplace that cats are sacred to spacemen.

3 Tell 'em to talk American like everyone else.

4 Ask 'em, "If you're so damn smart, how come our satellite dishes don't pick up any of *your* shows?"

5 Tell 'em we use steer manure for money, and offer 'em a couple truckloads full to get lost.

6 If they still don't make nice, bomb 'em back to Pluto.

"Okay- a few Pet-Earthrocks for the kids, some fuzzy dice for the ship, and **then** you can vaporize the planet!"

Pop goes the weasel

7

Postmodern reflections on the lawyer in popular culture

It seems hard to imagine a more maligned party of professionals than our learned friends, the lawyers. Entrusted with everything from our most cherished constitutional freedoms to our most reviled transgressions, they are a very easy and visible whipping post for every conceivable social ill. Lawyer-bashing is considered one of the healthier forms of spleen-venting in our culture. But it has an even more salutary, though less appreciated, effect. How we treat the legal paparazzi reveals even more about us than it does about them.

Consider this erudite diatribe:

> Careless of fame and of justice, they are described for the most part as ignorant and rapacious guides, who conducted their clients through a maze of expense, of delay and of disappointment, from whence, after a tedious series of years, they were at length dismissed, when their patience and fortune were almost exhausted.

This description of lawyers would seem perfectly at home in a newspaper editorial, a movie review, or a high-class watering hole almost anywhere in the world today. But it's more than 200 years old, and the subjects in question plied their trade more than 2000 years ago. It comes to us from the historian, Edward Gibbon, in his six-volume sizzler, *The Decline and Fall of the Roman Empire.*

So sullying the legal profession is older than the cracks on the seats in the Colosseum. Gibbon decried the deterioration of a calling that "had once been preserved as the sacred inheritance of the patricians," but had "fallen into the hands of freedmen and plebeians, who, with cunning rather than skill, exercised a sordid and pernicious trade."

This cuts to the crux of the bone that people have been picking with their advocates through the ages, although in a backhanded way. The author's scholarly snootiness about perceived lower classes taking up the law is the flip side of the beleaguered common man who downs a pint, wipes his mouth with his sleeve, and complains about them overpaid mouthpieces in their marble-tiled palaces.

> "The average, common man cannot understand this legal chicanery, and couldn't even if he devoted his whole mind to studying it, since he has to earn a living in the meanwhile."
>
> Thomas More, *Utopia* (1516)

The cloak of authority has always generated three attitudes: blind obedience, general acquiescence or defiant outrage. And it doesn't matter whether the garment is a black gown, a white wig or a paisley leisure suit. When Person A assumes a position of superior knowledge or other advantage over Person B, at least two things can happen. First, the relationship can be abused. And second, chances are at least one in three that B will get the urge to kick A all the way back to the end of the alphabet.

This urge can arise in a litany of different and even unintended ways. So many of us have heard of William Shakespeare's Dick in *Henry VI* uttering the immortal words, "The first thing we do, let's kill all the lawyers." This has become an endearing and enduring anthem for blaspheming God-fearing barristers and solicitors. But if the literati who quote the verse in scorn had actually read the play, they might have realized that Dick's words were dripping with irony, rather than venom. Like Thomas Hobbes, he believed that the alternative was chaos. (Today, of course, lawyers and chaos co-exist quite nicely.)

Charles Dickens was an unabashed champion of the weary and the downtrodden, many of whom could neither read nor afford to buy his work. He infused his popular writings with a robust blend of Victorian sentimentality and furious contempt for institutions and professions that he believed were exploiting the masses, instead of making life easier for them. You don't need a doctorate in English to fathom how the judicial system fared in novels like *Bleak House.* Suffice to say that the great author would have been heartened by a modern-day American Bar Association poll ranking lawyers somewhere between used car dealers and loan sharks in the public trust.

Fast-forwarding to the era of free speech—amplified a millionfold by an omniscient, pulsating, multimedia maze—we find similar, though thoroughly modern, expressions in everyday conversation (the ubiquitous and increasingly nasty lawyer jokes), books (titles like *Battered Lawyers, How to Survive a Lawyer* and *What to Do with Dead Lawyers,* and almost anything by John Grisham), film (the silly theatrics in *From the*

Hip, *My Cousin Vinnie* and *Trial and Error*) and television (the silly theatrics in the O.J. Simpson trial).

Let's face it. We live in an age where cynicism runs rampant, and media minions valiantly take up the mantle of "investigative" journalism practised in the wake of Watergate. The bigger they are, the harder they fall, and all that.

> "My attorney is brilliant. He can look at a contract and tell you in a minute if it's oral or written."
>
> Michael Iapoce, *A Funny Thing Happened on the Way to the Boardroom* (1988)

The rapiers take on a further sharpness in the great postmodern rat race. Urban neighbours often don't have the time or inclination to talk to each other. This is not exactly fertile breeding ground for a public relations campaign for lawyers.

Public trust was a lot easier in former generations, before technology accelerated the pace of everyday life to frenzied levels. People seemed to have so much more time then.

A popular perception of bygone days is that your lawyer was more likely an old family friend than a faceless, heartless suit who ranks your concerns behind his racquetball game, stock portfolio and Audi payments. Suing your legal adviser back then would have been as unthinkable as not suing her today. And the level of public discourse seemed *so* much more polite.

While financial pressures and rising consumer expectations lend some truth to the comparison, there's another side to the legal profession as well.

In the summer of 1994, the then president of the Canadian Bar Association, Cecilia Johnstone, made national headlines with an impassioned speech denouncing lawyer-bashing as a symptom of a culture of complaint. She praised the profession's strong work ethic, its varied volunteer efforts and its commitment to upholding the law and safeguarding our fundamental freedoms. And she told the association's 38,000 members that it was time for lawyers to stop apologizing for themselves.

It remains to be seen whether our popular culture will stop demanding an apology.

This won't happen overnight. As we have seen, lambasting legal counsel is neither new, nor original. It's a tradition as ancient as the profession itself. But don't shed a tear for our friends, the lawyers. Some think that any kind of recognition is better than being ignored.

Like any other vocation, the law has its leaders, innovators and risk-takers—folks that even Charles Dickens might admire. Naturally, it also harbours the moral sludge of society, some of whom get caught and punted publicly from the law society rolls. Then there's the great gaggle in the middle.

Most lawyers do not conduct crazed cross-examinations like Groucho's Rufus T. Firefly in *Duck Soup.* They do not become celebrities on the game show circuit like F. Lee Bailey. Their offices are likely not a front for the mob, as in *The Firm.* And they probably don't need a near-fatal bullet wound to reduce them to a near-vegetative state and reconstruct their personality into something resembling a human being, as in *Regarding Henry.*

"My daddy's a movie actor, and sometimes he plays the good guy and sometimes he plays the lawyer."

Malcolm Ford, preschool-aged son of actor Harrison Ford, quoted by David Halberstam in *Reader's Digest* (December, 1993)

Most lawyers are not Horace Rumpole, Perry Mason, *My Cousin Vinnie,* or even the kinder, gentler and airbrushed version that was Claire Huxtable.

Of course, the stereotypes in our popular culture have some basis in reality. They wouldn't be stereotypes if they didn't. But the naked, unvarnished truth is that many lawyers are fine human beings, and as a group, they are no different than anyone else.

It's only when we stop treating them as special or different that we'll ease up on bashing lawyers, and realize that they're subject to the same stresses, needs and temptations as everyone else.

If there is a lesson in the treatment of legal advocates in our popular culture, it's this: do unto thy lawyer as you would have others' lawyers do unto you.

Rules for eating at fancy restaurants

Source
Ollie Sherbaniuk

Occupation
Oilman

Residence
Calgary, Alberta

Motto
"You can't buy beer, only rent it."

Rules

1. Enter on the right foot. Look for one of them low-down metal bars to scrape the mud off your boots. If you don't see one, borrow the beefeater's hat.

2. Ignore anything that tells you to wait to be seated—especially in the can. Just take the bull by the horns and park it, pard.

3. Show some class. Anyone can order draft. Ask for a beer list and smile all knowing-like at the foreign section. Then order one of them "premium lagers."

4. Avoid your usual barroom colloquialisms, like "Kegger!", "More nachos over here!" and "Excuse my French."

5. Remember the code of the West. Have a conscience in there. Don't order no medallions unless you've actually won something. Like a rodeo prize, for instance.

6. If you're not man enough to empty your plate, ask for a doggy bag. But never—and I mean *never*—carry it out in your Stetson.

9

Test your Art Gallery Etiquette

GREETINGS AND WELCOME to a forum on the rules of acceptable behaviour in a cultural setting. This brief, yet helpful, quiz will test your Art Gallery Etiquette (AGE). Serious marks will be deducted from anyone who believes that gallery hangings should be replaced by lethal injections.

1. Your invitation to the opening of an exhibition of fetching etchings by Group of Seven contemporary Tom Thomson arrives 15 minutes before the show starts, and you discover that your little nephew has incinerated 98 per cent of your wardrobe, including all of your black wear. Your most appropriate course of action is to:

   (a) go buck naked and hope nobody notices
   (b) wear a barrel and spend the evening trolling for handouts
   (c) strap a bunch of Precambrian stones over your groin and go as a new form of birth control, the "Canadian Shield"
   (d) rent a canoe, drive out to the nearest lake and drown under mysterious circumstances.

2. On the way to the gallery, you learn that your date harbours a highly vocal distaste for any artwork not created, or at least strongly influenced, by Dr. Suess. Your first thought is:

    (a) a vow of celibacy
    (b) *Go, Dog, Go*
    (c) electroshock therapy
    (d) to go out back and play a game called Ring the Gack.

3. Much to your surprise, your date brings along two out-of-town visitors introduced to you as Aunt Frieda and Uncle Snidely, who think that visual art is some guy with 20-20 vision. You have three more stoplights to explain the history of art and its impact on Western civilization, touching on the Rembrandt school, the Bauhaus school and the school of hard knocks. Be brief.

4. As you gallop up the steps to the gallery, you notice that the entrance is patrolled by Uzi-toting storm troopers, and realize that you left your invitation to the opening in the soufflé that you baked the night before. Smelling your mounting fear, a Rambo-esque behemoth approaches you and snarls. Your response is to:

    (a) claim ownership of the gallery and wave him off indignantly
    (b) tell him that you'd love to personally hand him your invitation, but your Asian Flu has been acting up
    (c) smile weakly and request directions to the bus station
    (d) cry crocodile tears on his crocodile boots and crawl for mercy.

5. You are raptly ruminating over the choice of cheeses on the refreshment table when the person on your right slaps you on the back and throws up on your shoes. People start to stare. Your best course of action is to:

   (a) do the same thing to the person on your left, and start a wave
   (b) wish he had been a cubist and had simply gone, "Braque!"
   (c) try to imagine how the Cat in the Hat would have handled it
   (d) wonder what performance art was coming to.

6. The guest speaker announces her intention to exceed her allotted half-hour with a six-hour analysis of the importance of blue finger bowls to the works of Botticelli, El Greco and Hank Ketcham, the creator of *Dennis the Menace.* Discuss whether you would stay and listen out of politeness, or simply give her the finger bowl.

7. According to a recent survey of cultural literacy, four out of five people interviewed on frozen Canadian streets think that A.Y. Jackson is Michael and LaToya's kid sister, and three out of five think that Illingworth Kerr is the bloke from the old cooking show. And if that wasn't enough, the long-range forecast for Canadian culture calls for:

   (a) help
   (b) retroactive birth control
   (c) gusting winds with showers and highs of zero on the weekend
   (d) Dr. Suess.

8. Back at the gallery, your date, visibly shaken by an installation piece on the systemic eradication of the cellular telephone, dashes into the appropriate rest room, never to return. At that point, you should:

   (a) sign up for one of those convenient monthly plans while you still can
   (b) sidle up to the nearest statue and tell it all your troubles
   (c) pick up dozens of those weird free postcards in the lobby and mail them to former flames, inquiring about the prospect of reconciliation
   (d) wonder what the hell you're going to do with Aunt Frieda and Uncle Snidely.

9. While wandering aimlessly through an exhibit called *Our Friend the Emu,* you encounter a stranger in a black trench coat, who apprises you of his intention to avenge his bad childhood by dropping the world's largest water balloon from the balcony overlooking the main hall. You have 60 seconds to deflate his idea, or at least convince him that it won't hold water.

10. And now for the tie-breaker. To cap a perfect evening, you accidentally walk through a life-sized realist painting depicting a corridor, and spend two confused hours wandering around, wearing the canvas, before the police arrive and arrest you for creating a public disturbance. Your best strategy is to:

    (a) bet the officers that you look better in canvas than they do

(b) demand that they read you your lefts as well as your rights
(c) inquire as to the firmness of the mattresses at the remand centre
(d) ask the judge for leniency because you were framed.

Thank you for playing. See you at the galleries.

Rules for attending opening night at the opera

Source
Mabel Baganbaru

Occupation
Owner, Fab Four Forever
Memorabilia Shoppe
& Market Garden

Residence
Palembang, Indonesia

Motto
"Bingo, Ringo."

Rules

1 When the orchestra enters, stand up, pelt them with jelly beans and scream "Yeah, yeah, yeah!" until you wet your pants.

2 Liven up the usual blue rinse colognes by exuding the exciting new Fabergé fragrance, *Eau de Cavern Wall,* or the classic "natural" scent, *I Am the Walrus.*

3 Conventional opera glasses are totally non-gear, man. Instead, look at the girl with kaleidoscope eyes.

4 Record the first letter of every ninth word sung onstage. They may spell out clues to prove that Paul really is dead. (Don't let his last few albums fool you.)

5 Whenever a character is killed onstage, light a candle and sing *Give Peace a Chance.*

6 During intermission, tell everyone within earshot the real reason behind *The Beatles Anthology:* that Yoko was going broke-o.

Romeo and Juliet (or, Magnum PEI)

11

A contemporary Canadian treatment of a timeless tale of lost love and un-consummated billings

IF YOU ARE A ROMANTIC AT HEART, you may recall something of the fellow known in Elizabethan beatnik circles as Bill the Shake, and his homage to history's hardest-luck lovers, who dared to break the rules. But being busy in mind, you may not know that the playwright purloined the plot from a third-century Ephesian writer named Xenophon. Continuing this defiance of originality, the tale transposes further from the Bard of Avon to the boardrooms of Avonlea.

Act I

Dawn breaks beyond the high-rise bearing the Prince Edward Island offices of Alpha, Romeo & Ferrari ("ARF"), specialists in (you guessed it) motor vehicle law. A driven junior associate, Romeo Romeo, idles around the accounts receivable department, weeping.

"It's that licensing mega-file he's working on," puffs his pal, Ben Volvo. "That accursed Sloop crew started a real row this time." Indeed, the litigation is the latest in a long raft of rows between Avonlea's two biggest law firms: a log-jam over the new link between PEI and mainland Canada. ARF is in favour of it, swimming in the resulting file traffic, but their arch-rivals at Sloop John Itbee ("SJI"), with their decreasingly swamped maritime law practice, are currently less than buoyed by the notion of boats yielding to cars.

For Romeo Romeo, the lawsuit is almost as cathartic as having to explain his twin first and last names. (At his birth, his father had but a moment between court appearances to devise a name, and apparently drew a blank.)

The suit flows from a nasty accident—a car disembarking from a ferry crashing into a flashing dock light, causing the lamppost to sail through the windshield of the driver, Don Yon, and sullying his best ascot. This prompts Romeo to ask the defendant's officer of record, "What light through Yon window breaks?" When opposing counsel Juliet Itbee objects on the basis of his failure to use iambic pentameter, their eyes meet for the first time. They decide to damn their respective firms' feuding and launch their own practice. Juliet undertakes to draft the partnership documents.

Act II

Overwhelmed by the colossal lark of it all, Romeo confesses his secret to a retired judge, Larry Fryer, who agrees to review their closing agenda "just for the hell of it."

Meanwhile, a specialist in houseboat leases at SJI named Ty Bulkhead charts the demise of his hated opponent, Romeo, who had smoked him in a hotly contested race for chairman of the local potato marketing board. Bulkhead fires off a complaint with the law society against Romeo for appearing in court in an ill-fitting gown. "Measure for measure...not," says Ty's supporting affidavit. "It may not be as you like it, but this comedy of errors is much ado about nothing," is Romeo's playful rejoinder.

Under cover of darkness and plastic ferns, Romeo and Juliet rendezvous secretly with Larry Fryer, who pronounces on the spiritual propriety of the closing agenda. "By the power vested in me, I bless this union," he declares, toasting the event with a triple-thick shake.

Act III

While Romeo and his favourite client, a Ford-Mercutio dealer, steer through some garageman's liens, Bulkhead swears an information alleging that one of Romeo's witnesses had an accident during a rigorous cross-examination, and that Romeo had failed to remain on the scene. Romeo's persuasive comeback: "All the world's a stage, and I've been in every scene of this thing so far, so go soak your head."

With the wind knocked out of his sails, Bulkhead pulls some strings and ropes Ford-Mercutio into bankruptcy. A sputtering Romeo runs over to a friend of a friend, and gets Bulkhead beached from all of his files. Bulkhead is cut loose from SJI, and is last seen scraping barnacles off rotting poop decks washed up on the red rocks of Cavendish.

When the authorities get wind of this, Romeo is shifted to the inactive list and forced to flee the jurisdiction. After he spends a fortnight and three fortdays crying on Father Larry's shoulder, the old judge sends him a stiff dry cleaning bill.

To complicate matters, Juliet's father and firm patriarch, Figby Itbee, announces that as of April 1, he is pairing her on all her files with Guy Paris, a junior partner whom he calls "a hull of a good catch." Though Juliet accepts this with Grace (her legal assistant), the sinking fate of the proposed partnership makes her stern. Bowing to overhead winds, her colleagues urge her not to go overboard and fall behind on billings.

Act IV

Juliet tells Larry Fryer that she would not love being with Paris in the springtime, preferring to go adrift with Romeo. Sensing a chance to end the feud and free up time for more golf, the old judge proposes a daring plan. First, Juliet will feign burnout to gain time to complete the partnership paperwork, which she will stow in her firm's dead filing room. Then Romeo will apply for an immigrant visa and get night work with the janitorial outfit charged with sweeping up at SJI (under a *nom de broom,* of course), and pick up and sign the agreements. When the deal is done, the pair can claim protection under an obscure rule of canon law, and practise together in peace.

Act V

Unfortunately, Romeo misconstrues Larry Fryer's fax (which is in Latin) and overlooks the part about showing up in disguise. He careens into SJI's dead filing room and runs into Guy Paris. When Paris recognizes him, Romeo advises Paris that Paris' BMW was repossessed, which automatically disqualifies him from practising law. Paris sulks off with dead files in tow. By then, Romeo is so far out of control that he cannot find the file containing Juliet's work. Assuming she wants to back out of the deal, he panics and is found early the next morning, accelerating down the halls in his shorts, flinging files into the air and shouting *Bess, You is My Woman Now* at the top of his lungs.

Within a half-hour, senior partner Othello Sloop serves Romeo with a non-molestation order and a permanent disbarment notice, both adroitly pulled off the precedent shelf and signed by a hastily awoken judge. Juliet returns to work just in time to see Romeo led away by police. Heartbroken, she pulls a painting off the wall and breaks the canvas over his head, with the words, "Romeo Romeo, wear poor art now, Romeo." Having purchased all of the firm's paintings, Sloop takes the brush-off personally, turns colour and fluidly strokes Juliet off the letterhead.

When the dust settles, ARF and SJI realize that if they drove their associates to such ruin, they must be on similar wavelengths after all. They start up merger talks, and combine their expertise to conduct cases of collisions between boats and vehicles around the new Confederation Bridge.

Romeo and Juliet are never heard from again, but are remembered fondly in haunting ballads, sung with zesty relish at lobster suppers in church basements across the island.

Rules for romancing your heart's desire

Source
Bobby Bower

Occupation
Grain elevator "leg" operator

Residence
Plum Coulee, Manitoba

Motto
"Just give 'er."

Rules

1 Plow her name into the biggest wheat field you can find, eh?

2 Buy her her weight in back bacon.

3 Take her to the heart of Canada—the underpass at Portage and Main—and explain how much it reminds you of her.

4 Get Don Cherry to give her not one, but *two* big thumbs-up during "Coach's Corner."

5 Take her out to the lake, eh? Then like, crank up some BTO and ask her if she's ever heard the Pierre Berton quote about Canadians makin' out in canoes.

6 Offer her your very last brewski.

The answer to all of Canada's problems

13

Hope your constitution is up to it

It is no accident that the biggest recurring headache in Canadian history concerns the rules by which we play at being a country—that is, our inability to agree on them. As our ultimate set of rules, our constitution languished as a British statute for more than a century before Mr. Trudeau brought it home as a retirement project in 1982, over the objections of his own province, and after a withering courtroom battle with the rest of them.

Since then, we have weathered the breach of the Meech Lake Accord, the piercing of the Pearson Accord, the charlatanry over the Charlottetown Accord and an addendum referendum, which, as pundits note, may neverendum. But it has to stop somewhere. So here, at no public expense whatsoever, are 10 proposals for a new constitutional order, aimed at squelching the squealing once and for all. Kindly give them the serious consideration that they deserve.

Symbol

The first thing that any new order needs is a symbol for rallying purposes, and a flag to put it on, because flags look good in parades. The maple leaf is all right, but it doesn't grow from coast to coast.

A more fair choice is the fig leaf. It doesn't grow anywhere in Canada. But it does stand for modesty and discretion, attributes so quintessentially Canadian that they prevail even when the nation teeters on the brink of chaos. (The Americans have a civil war. We set up discounted "unity" airfares, sew a huge flag and stage non-denominational prayer services.) Another point in favour of the fig is its well-documented laxative properties, which should remind everyone of the dangers of further constitutional discourse.

Capital

Although Ottawa is a charming place to visit, it has become a symbol of a Bytown age which many of us would love to get Rideau. It was a sorry symptom of the old order that many Canadians never saw the place where their tax dollars went to die.

We could cure all of that in the new Canada with a rotating seat of government. Each year would see a new capital from a different part of the country, whatever it turns out to be. The month of August could be set aside for moving legislators and their staff by railway handcar. This would foster physical fitness, curb commuting costs and revive the romance of the rails. Both arduous elections and the messy mandatory retirement issue would be replaced, at least in the federal public service, by a more holistic process of natural selection. If you can't complete the trip to the next capital, you're out of the game.

Leader

A clear flaw in the old Canada was this nonsense of party politics, where the only ideology common to any group with a minuscule chance of electoral success was seizing power on Parliament Hill. In an age when the medium (as opposed to the rare or well done) is the message, we need more. Marshall

McLuhan twigged onto this; Ronald Reagan branched out his acting career with it; and Andy Warhol used it to play us for saps.

The ideal leader for life of the new order would be Louis Del Grande, an ingenious, balding prophet with black glasses, whose hilarious small screen asides stated the Canadian cause more eloquently than a tuqueful of Royal Commissions, and at a fraction of the cost. Sure, the guy hails from New Jersey. But after siphoning torrents of Canadian comic talent southward, isn't it about time our good neighbours sent us something more in return than Beavis and Butthead?

National broadcaster

As a hallmark of the old, faded order, the CBC (or what's left of it) would of course have to go. In an age where today's cutting-edge technology is tomorrow's rusted-out Ginsu knife, radio and television are palpably passé.

We would move to the New Order Personal Headspace (NOPH) broadcasting system, melding yogic karma and fibre optic cable into an hourly, high-speed transmission of good vibes into your home, job site or prison cell. Think of it as the ultimate sound bite: no words at all. Just send endorphins, and let the rest take care of itself. Traditional news anchors would be thrown overboard. Disk jockeys would be ridden out of town. Golden, Zen-like silence would rule the airwaves. And we'd create a nifty new national catchphrase: "NOPH said."

Language

With the demise of the old Canada and official bilingualism, we'd have to quell a cacophony of competing interests. Rather than breathe new life into the old fog, the new order would clear the air with a new language policy guaranteed not to offend any group—more than any other, at least.

In the spirit of populism, multiculturalism and Dadaism, the new order would boast an "Official Language of the Month." Linguistic lobby groups would be invited to present an evening of poetry-reading, folk dancing and ethnic cleansing to the Official Language Ministry (the "Lingo Gringos") every fourth Tuesday at an open amphitheatre in the capital, wherever it may happen to be. The language of the winning entry would be granted official status for the following month, with a further month's extension if an encore is called for on the audience applause meter.

Animal

The beaver has always been depicted as unobtrusive and industrious, highly prized attributes in the old Canada. However, it is also a pesky rodent that contributes to deforestation and blocks the waterways of the land, a dammed nuisance to many.

We should up the ante with a more gregarious symbol that tells the world that we *really* mean business: the pit bull. Why spend time stoically rebuilding a dynamited dam when you can bark a little, scare the pants off people and attract a lot of free advertising?

Motto

A mare usque ad mari is in a dead language that only posh private school graduates can understand. But the new order, presumably a patchwork of disparate regions, would demand a more accessible and geographically accurate motto: *Here and there.* Other options include *Puckland, Politeness-R-Us* and *The Eh? Team.*

Sport

Every country needs a national sport to whip its citizens into a xenophobic frenzy and bring some spark into their drab lives. Scholarly texts told us that the old Canada had lacrosse. Many thought that lacrosse was la big, tall thing on top of la hill in Montréal. No wonder the country was falling apart. And although ice hockey enjoyed some popularity, it has gone Hollywood, and most pros won't accept Canadian dollars until Tinseltown itself freezes over.

The perfect national sport for the new order is hopscotch. It can be played all year round, indoors, outdoors or, in classically Canadian fashion, half-in and half-out. You don't need genetic counselling, jockstraps or practices at 7:00 a.m. on Saturdays. And it provides mental stimulation by requiring participants to jump to conclusions.

Currency

The Canuck buck has degenerated into a pale imitator of its Yankee counterpart. Although the Loonie was a truly inspired choice, the new order would replace it and the other bucolic motifs now gracing Canadian currency with images of specially crafted and focus-tested cartoon characters.

If some of the most beloved figures in Canada are Finnegan the Dog, Rusty the Rooster and Jerome the Giraffe, then surely we are ready for coinage bearing the likeness of Toddy the Toadstool, Faron the Ferret and Plato the Platypus. The coins would instantly become collector's items, and international sales of the accompanying dolls, drawers and dental floss (fronted by the obligatory "educational" TV series, *Name that Scat*) would drop an anvil on any threat of a trade deficit.

Anthem

An annoying shortcoming of our old national ode is that it never even dented the *Billboard Hot 100.* With a little promotion and the right label, a new order anthem could take the masses by storm and boost the national coffers, offsetting the need for a further tax increase for at least 15 minutes.

Such an anthem would give national unity a shot in the arm (if not the head) by appealing to camps as wide-ranging as whistling lumberjacks, placid paper-pushers and neo-nihilists sporting enough chains to start their own drawbridge. Possible titles for the new chart-topper would be *Early Morning Grain* (sung by Gordon Lightfoot), *Snowblurred* (sung by Anne Murray) and *Clap for the Pit Bull* (sung by The Guess Who, if they ever stop suing each other).

Oy, Canada

So, gentle reader, the next time someone drones on about Canada going the way of the pogo stick, don't lose hop.

Jump into the spirit of the new order by imagining that you're flying the fig; dancing to a patriotic downbeat from your headset as you pass Louis del Grande walking a pit bull; picking up some great vibes *Here and there;* and watching a cheery round of hopscotch in your home town between two Esperanto-speaking MPs on a rest break during a ride on the rails. And hey, try to snag the coin that they're using in place of the now defunct rock. It's a collector's item!

If none of this scares you further, then you'll never need to weep for the good ship Canada. Like so many, you'll have missed the boat altogether.

O CANADA, OUR FIG LEAF-BEREFT LAND / WE SAY A "NOPH" LED BY LOUIS
DEL GRANDE / WITH
SNOWBLURRED HEARTS
IN LANGUAGE MYSTÈRE
AND WITH PIT BULL-
LIKE FINESSE / FROM

HERE AND THERE O
CANADA / WITH
NO FIXED CAPIT-
AL ADDRESS / GOD
KEEP OUR COINS

MADE 'TOONFULLY / WE
SHOUT "EN GARDE" WHILE
PLAYING HOPSCOTCH, WE /
CROW, "CANADA, WE GIVE
A FIG, MAIS OUI!"

Rules for proper parliamentary debate

Source
Bertram "Billy" Billabong

Occupation
Adventure tour guide

Residence
Toowoomba, Australia

Motto
"Cowabunga!"

Rules

1. Check all your bowie knives at the door.
2. You can't call anyone a liar. But it's okay to refer to an honourable member as a sloth-sucking, mealy-mouthed, weak-kneed wombat.
3. If there is a motion, grab your binoculars. You might see an endangered species!
4. Be nice to seconders. They try harder, mate.
5. Avoid breaking bottles over your neighbour's head, leaping over your desk and starting bench-clearing brawls. Express your displeasure in more sporting ways, like hauling in wheelbarrows full of dingo dung.
6. Never speak out of turn, unless your opponent starts cackling like a kookaburra. Then you get to shoot the pesky little loudmouth.

How law and words go together like tar and feathers

15

Of blather, fustian gabble and folderol stultiloquence, hereunto annexed

WORDS. SEEMINGLY SIMPLE, yet laden with all of the subtextual subtleties and complexities that the human condition can muster. As our leading instrument of communication, words have evolved from the primal pleasures of the prehistoric grunt to the cyberspatial vagaries of "Netiquette."

Rudyard Kipling called the word the most powerful drug used by mankind, leaving latter-day, inclusive sorts to speculate on the potency of narcotics favoured by womankind. Aldous Huxley credited our use of words with both our rise above the brutes and our sinking to the level of the demons. Not to be outdone, the Brothers Gibb, before their vistas were multiplied by the miracle of polyester, sang that words were all they had to take our heart away.

Although many have had their way with words through the ages, few have wreaked havoc with them as much as our learned confreres and consoeurs in the business of creating, enforcing and interpreting the laws by which we are governed. If brevity is truly the soul of wit, as Shakespeare hammered home in *Hamlet,* then these unfortunates must surely rank among the most witless wonders ever to grace God's good, green earth.

Consider the early custom of paying lawyers by the word—a practice analogous to paying armed insurgents by the shell fragment, and a viable cause of the evolution from the simple, if occasionally brutal, elegance of the Code of Hammurabi in 1750 BC to the latest manifestation of Canada's income tax legislation, a labyrinthine vortex of flapdoodling flumadiddle so massive that not even the Minotaur-mangler, Theseus, would touch it with a 10-foot thesaurus.

Time was, so the story goes, that lawyers' robes contained pouches for obliging clients to replenish with silver whenever their counsel exceeded the agreed word count. (Presumably, disgruntled clients, bored judges and struggling chiropractors would have lobbied the royal mint to use a heavier metal, like lead.)

To modern, popular culture-caked minds, this conjures up images of fuzzy, battery-operated, little bunnies with little word-o-meters in their tummies, winding down in mid-argument, only to be re-energized by frantic clients vaulting over the bar and restocking the pouch before both momentum and case drown in a sea of ineloquent silence. But to the paparazzi of the day, it must have made eminent sense to tie quantity to quality, along with such inspired notions as killing gypsies, sending kids to coal mines and sailing off the end of the world.

Fragments of this ethos remain with us in the venerable "boiler plate" brandished by stressed-out solicitors in agreements so putatively comprehensive that they make *War and Peace* look like *Hop on Pop.* This is why lawyers' abrupt adherence to "plain language" is one of life's lovely ironies. Today, they are crusading to save us from the officious gibberish that someone decided was required to protect our rights in a litigious world.

More to the point, they are saving us from themselves.

This kinder and gentler breed of law also rears its head in that once-stable staple of our legal system, the adversarial process. Fading fast are the diverting days where indignant barristers apoplectically went toe to toe, and threatened to blow the other's case clear out of the courtroom, if not to the nether regions of each other's anatomy. Today, steeped in New Age mediation techniques and cloying homilies like "win-win," they pass themselves off as *alternative dispute resolution specialists,* geared fearlessly, once again, to saving us from themselves.

Another emerging tactic, particularly among the more densely populated firms, is to hire clever specialists in public relations, marketing and communications, to supply the right words to convince consumers that lawyers are not as tough on the system as, say, an advanced case of tuberculosis.

In all fairness, the law is not the only business to succumb to what the British linguist, Geoffrey Hughes, aptly called "verbicide and semantic engineering." The medical, advertising and computer trades have done so with comparable aplomb, and governments are notorious for coming up with new words which are designed to communicate, but ultimately achieve the opposite result. Our black-robed and designer label-clad friends are no better or worse than anyone else.

But legalese rankles common folks more than any other linguistic perversions because they see it as a mercenary tactic to bar their understanding of the legal system, and to safeguard lawyers' monopoly over it. Dredging up medieval jabberwocky in a modern lease or will can cloud matters for a client, but it clearly reveals the responsible lawyer's true regard for the client as an individual, not to mention a certain laxity when it comes to discarding precedents predating the Franco-Prussian War.

On the other hand, verbicide does have benefits. It may well be a step up from the school of law practiced by Chico Marx in *A Night at the Opera,* when he hands Groucho a blank contract for signature. (When Groucho indignantly declares that he can't have his client sign it in that form, Chico shrugs and promises to add the words later, after the contract is signed.)

Another reason that legalese gets on the public's case is that unlike most other fields, words have always been the straw that stirs the legal drink. Consider the volumes brimming with horrifyingly hard-fought, protracted and expensive litigation over such burning questions as whether women are persons. Imagine the mountains of time, effort and resources sacrificed at the judicial altar on such profundities as whether Dobermans are tax-deductible security systems for home-based businesses. Bound—but unfortunately, not gagged—books bearing titles such as *Words and Phrases Judicially Considered* are a chilling testament to quixotic pursuits of defining words that everyone thought they already understood. Surely all of this energy could have been better spent on ridding the world of greater evils, like nuclear waste, infomercials and athlete's foot.

The law seems to recognize this, for the usual goulash of altruistic and self-serving reasons. Practitioners of legalese appear more disposed to the idea that bringing the law to the people is a Good Thing. Plain language, mediation and increasing efforts at public outreach suggest that for the legal business, customer service and self-preservation may be the ultimate marriage of convenience.

In a sense, the legal system is grappling with the challenge described by S.I. Hayakawa in a 1979 essay called *Language and Learning,* "to overthrow the tyranny of words by looking beyond words to the complex realities for which they stand."

Whether the law's architects, construction workers and hangers-on can manage the transition from tyranny to reality will be the measure of the system's continued relevance, in a world where people demand increasing openness and clarity from their institutions.

Whether anyone will actually *care* about any of this will be the measure of their success.

Rules for discriminating grocery-shopping

Source
Pierrette Jollicoeur

Occupation
Professor of linguistics

Residence
Trois-Pistoles, Québec

Motto
"A word to the wise—and it had better be in French."

Rules

1. Check the labels carefully, and report any infractions to the language police without delay. Keep a special watch for missing accents, obvious syntactical errors and anglicisms cleverly coded in Pig Latin.

2. Beware of words like *éclair, crêpes* and *escargots,* which look French, but may actually have been intended as English.

3. Show your pride by buying Québecois products exclusively—even when picking up snacks for your annual winter trip to Florida.

4. Stock up on staples like French dressing, French fries and French doors.

5. Bilingual packaging is acceptable—French and joual.

6. Any purchase of English muffins is punishable by immediate expulsion to Mississauga, with no possibility of parole for 25 double-coupon Tuesdays.

Talkin' politically correct blues

17

A number from the act

LISTEN FOLKS, IT'S ALL AROUND
And what a profound effect
The wonders of our language abound
When we're talkin' politically correct.

I was born with pale skin
And homely, too
Was told that couldn't be retracted
But now they tell me with much ado
I'm non-minority and
    non-pulchritudinally impacted.

Oh, when your heart and soul
Hang over the line of scrimmage
You're not fat
You have a horizontal body image.

And if you stretch the truth
With facts invented
You're not a liar,
You're just ethically disoriented.

If your forehead's rising
And your bifocals unbalanced
You're not bald and blind
You're hair-disadvantaged
And optically challenged.

And if you screw up real good
Not long for the work force
You've achieved a deficiency
And your position's outsourced.

If you're expecting a child
Whether planned or perchance
You're not pregnant
You're parentally enhanced.

And if you're dumb as a post
And your mind's a mess
You're not stupid
Just cerebrally oppressed.

So when you're getting on
Had your face lifted
You ain't old
Just chronologically gifted.

And at the final checkout
When you reach the pearly fence
You won't be dead
Just terminally inconvenienced!

SACRED TO THE
MEMORY OF
N. "CON"
VENIENCED
1945 - 1998
HORIZONTALLY
CHALLENGED
NO MORE

Rules for networking around a funeral pyre

Source
Jennifer B. Galt

Occupation
President, Elite Power Marketing Concepts Inc.

Residence
Toronto, Ontario

Motto
"Your latest product could put you over the top—with the right spin."

Rules

1. Arrive early, to make sure you get a place where everyone can see you, and that someone else gets the chair with the broken leg.

2. Carry three day planners, two cellphones and a stack of "Hot Rush" message slips, to build your mystique.

3. Tell the mourners you share their pain. Then ask if it's okay to share business cards.

4. Always send the right message. Take out a huge billboard ad expressing your sympathies to the family and the entire community, and make sure you include a smiling photo, your client satisfaction guarantee and your 1-800 number.

5. Make conversation, and work in your expertise. Discuss the village undertaker's potential to double his business with an aggressive, but tasteful, media buying strategy.

6. Avoid cultural faux pas, like pulling out a cigarette when the pyre is lit and asking, "Anyone mind if I smoke, too?"

Seven solid signs that your boss is burning out

19

Watching out for your favourite authority figure

1
Comes to morning meetings in bathrobe and fuzzy slippers

2
Signs your annual performance appraisal in brown crayon

3
Constantly consults telephone book to confirm that he/she is still listed

4
During critical decision-making moments, turns to ugly stuffed rat on desk and asks, "What do *you* figure, Ollie?"

5
Takes to growing illicit relaxants hidden among legitimate office plants

6
Flies into a rage whenever anyone mentions Henri Matisse or any other Fauvists

7
Can only communicate with family and friends through action requests and inter-office memos

Rules for keeping a clean coffee room

Source
Miguel Pomdetérres

Occupation
Generalissimo Second Class, People's Liberation Army

Residence
Bucaramanga, Colombia

Motto
"Ask questions first—but shoot before hearing the answers."

Rules

1 Hygienic standards are important. Discard coffee filters after every hundred uses, whether they need it or not.

2 Leave all soiled machetes at the door. It helps keep the maggot count down.

3 When the fan breaks down, please refrain from ventilating the room with machine gun blasts.

4 Be nice to the janitor. Once the junta falls, he could be Minister of Defence.

5 Anyone uttering even one Juan Valdez joke must mop the floor with his own spit.

6 Out of respect for others, please limit your intake of the Colombian whitener.

How to renovate your home and stay emotionally erect

21

A guide to the opiate of the suburban bourgeoisie

LIKE LIFE ITSELF, home renovation has built itself into a multi-billion-dollar industry. In our suburban paradise, driveways sprouting dumpsters have come to rival tulips as a sure sign of spring, and lawn flamingos as a sure sign of middle age.

As so many well-meaning homeowners have found, renovating a home is a microcosm of life's intricate and infinite web of logistics, glories and pratfalls. No wonder really smart divorce lawyers send anonymous gifts of wallpaper to married households as a business development tool.

The Canadian Home Builders' Association calls home renovation the fastest growing part of the housing industry. They're not just coughing up a drainpipe.

A quick tour of cyberspace dredges up a plethora of players. There's Macka's Home Improvement Inc. in Western Australia (no mention of house calls). Folks are invited to mosey on down to Jim the Home Improvement Specialist at the Liberty State Bank, somewhere in Middle America. Articles abound on topics like "Understanding the relationship of the bathroom to the rest of your home." And homeowners share their home improvement experiences in a manner befitting ancient mariners spinning epic sagas of the high seas centuries ago.

Clearly, this is a very big deal. And it's being driven by more than just another pretty facade.

Experts point to social, demographic, economic and environmental factors. They also point to shooting stars, traffic accidents and cute Lego displays in toy departments. And when they're done pointing, they talk about some interesting stuff.

The last recession has receded into memory.

Home-based businesses are proliferating like sunflowers at a Van Gogh retrospective.

The ever-dominant flower power generation has entered the sandwich generation, where their parents come back home and their kids don't leave. This creates what's called "multi-generational housing" or "a colossal pain in the ass," depending on who's doing the calling.

There's a growing sensitivity to designing living space for people with various kinds of disabilities. For example, many new homes feature low roofs for the vertically challenged, and soothing portraits instead of mirrors for the cosmetically challenged.

The home security market has opened up to the masses, and is expanding at an alarming rate. Allied to this is the widening web of wires winding through today's homes.

Concerns about energy consumption and "sick" buildings have spawned a slew of health audits, retrofits and raging debates on the ins and outs of insulation—and exactly why it has to be such a perfectly horrid shade of pink.

So how does one deal with it all? Here, at no extra charge to you, the reader, are four golden rules of home renovation, as sacrosanct as any that apply to the art of surviving in this dumpster-happy world of ours.

Make a plan, Stan

The initial hurdle is deciding just exactly what kind of renovations you want. A two-holer for the guest bathroom? A new high-ceilinged studio for levitating? Or maybe something even more ambitious. Consider the needs of the entire household, and the implications for not only today, but for as far ahead as next week.

Logistics and ergonomics are important, but don't neglect the fiscal side. The Appraisal Institute of Canada says that the average potential return on common renovation projects ranges from more than 70 per cent for kitchens and bathrooms, and 52 per cent for finished basements, down to 35 per cent for home office conversions and 16 per cent for swimming pools. Presumably, your payback on a sale of your home would be even less for add-ons like Italian marble urinals, flying buttresses or cheesy mermaid murals.

Gather the information that you need. Get the word from professional associations on the key issues. Or better yet, jump into it with both feet and get a whole sentence. Maybe even two.

Loiter around show homes disguised as Bill Gates. When agents ask if they can help you, tell them you're looking for an add-on in the 80,000-square-foot range. Infiltrate trade shows. Hang around hardware stores and ogle socket sets. Scan handy publications. Talk with sources you can trust. Consult the I Ching.

If appropriate, check your eligibility for aids like homeowner or rental residential rehabilitation assistance programs. Of course, your house may be beyond rehabilitation. Mine is a hard-core case. I tried a quick and dirty paint job as a deterrent, but it will never veer from its criminal ways. So I seek solace in the old proverb, "A happy home is a healthy home—send your house to the doctor once a year."

Find the right folks for you

Choosing a renovator is a lot like getting married. Doing the job properly involves checking things like how well they present themselves and communicate; their track record; the company they keep; how they deal with problems; whether their price is out of line; and whether they leave the toilet seat up.

Beware of putative professionals who scorn business cards, talk to invisible companions, or show up for work with nothing more than a sledgehammer and a big, dopey grin. A lousy choice will break your heart, while the right one can save you valuable recovery time on the coronary ward.

Of course, if you're a handy sort, you can hire yourself and save a lot of chicken dancing. But if you're like me, make sure that your health care premiums are paid up, and that your working schedule coincides with the business hours of the nearest drop-in medical clinic.

Cover your assets

A major benefit of renovating your home is the opportunity for a figurative—and if you *really* screw up, a literal—crash course on our legal system. Once you climb the ladder, the full panoply of legal possibilities awaits you under the first removable ceiling tile.

Your initial encounter will be the law of contract. Perhaps the greatest piece of legal wisdom of all time is the deathless doublespeak from movie mogul Sam Goldwyn about a verbal contract not being worth the paper it's written on.

Indeed, our neighbourhoods and courtrooms are littered with the debris of conflicts among a litany of defiant contractors, irate zoning authorities, frustrated suppliers and harried homeowners that would make the MGM lion long for the considerably less painful, and certainly less costly, anguish of Androcles' thorn. Perhaps the most redeemable benefit of sacrificing forests to record our earthly musings is that it provides a forum to focus on a shared understanding of our respective rights and obligations.

Unless that ironclad, 100-per cent, cross-my-heart-and-hope-to-die warranty is written down somewhere, it may rival Moses' missing commandments as the most sought-after truth in Christendom. On an only mildly more secular note, the omnipotent deities at Revenue Canada tend to favour receipts when home-based businesses try to deduct that new deck—er, *air-enhanced client conference and debriefing centre.*

Other exciting areas of the law can surface, triggered by everything from exploding furnaces (products liability), stiffed cement contractors (builders' liens) and hung-over neighbours crashing into ill-planned overhangs (zoning), to odious odours emanating from that new abattoir add-on (nuisance), larger than life lawn ornaments shaped like Elvis Presley in his heftier years (intentional infliction of nervous shock), and vase-throwing disputes between pipe-fitters and interior decorators over the placement of air ducts (assault, battery).

It'll cost you

The Canadian Real Estate Association recommends that people spend $1000 each year on keeping up their abodes. One might liken this to dragoons of dentists advising us to celebrate every Thanksgiving with a root canal, or maybe even an arsonists' league urging us to support our friends in the lighter fluid industry. But as in life, it's tough to escape the financial arena.

As loathsome as budgeting may be, it's not an entire waste of time for home renovations. You may not know the damage at the outset, but a ballpark figure of what you're prepared to dole out will make life easier for your contractor, your banker and your aromatherapist.

Then decide where you will get the dough. If you're short, then friendly loans officers will dazzle you with a variety of lines of credit, mortgages, home equity loans and personal loans (but never *im*personal loans)—anything to help their team win a paid day off in their institution's latest employee productivity competition. Don't overlook other avenues for quick cash, like obliging acquaintances, loan sharks and petty theft.

Home renovations present a nifty slice of life. Back in the mid-19th century, the retired American president, John Quincy Adams, proffered this perspective on everyone's ultimate home renovation project:

> "I inhabit a weak, frail and decayed tenement,
> battered by the winds and broken in on by the storms.
> And from all I can learn, the landlord does not
> intend to repair."

Good luck in all of your repairs.

Rules for selling Tupperware door to door

Source
Ziad El-Raqq

Occupation
Freelance mercenary/terrorist

Residence
Giarabub, Lybia

Motto
"May your beard ever grow long and your detonator fuse never grow short."

Rules

1. Fortune only affords a single opportunity to make a lasting first impression. Introduce yourself to homeowners by spelling out your name in hot lead on the aluminum siding.

2. Arouse sympathy by displaying photographs of your 12 wives, along with advertisements from the *Tripoli Plain Dealer* indicating the high cost of veils and formless, full-length female clothing.

3. Vehemently deny that your manufacturer also sells plastic explosives to terrorist organizations. Denounce this filthy fabrication as the work of your arch-competitors, those pasty-skinned, Nike-mongering Yankee hyenas.

4. Provide a list of satisfied customers who have not been blown to bits in Israeli airliners.

5. Remind reluctant customers of your new, coffin-sized product. Politely, but firmly, stress that the Locked-in Freshness™ feature is guaranteed to confuse coroners as to the time of the occupant's death.

6. Reveal that your commissions are pooled, and that your conversation is being monitored very closely by six of your trigger-happy sales associates.

All spin the family

23

Charting the future of our first den of rules

"THE FIRST WOULD BE OUR FAMILY. Your family, my family—which is composed of an immediate family of a wife and three children, a larger family with grandparents and aunts and uncles. We all have our family, whichever that may be."

Danforth J. Quayle, candidate for vice-president of the United States, in a campaign speech to schoolchildren in Virginia, 1988

Since the dawn of time, our deepest thinkers have devoted gazillions of grey cells to dissecting society's most basic building block. As our first box along the organizational chart of life, the family has always reflected the rules, priorities and peccadillos of its time and place. In just four decades, we have bounced, pinball-style, from the Nelsons, the Kramdens, the Cleavers and the Bradys to the Bunkers, the Huxtables, the Bundys and the Simpsons. No wonder we're so confused.

Shifting demographics, shrinking after-tax incomes, rising divorce rates, something resembling equal working opportunities for women, and lapsed parenting have combined to rock the family boat. So how will this venerable vessel fare in the wave of change sweeping us over the gurgling brink of a new millennium?

Invoking the spirits of shamuses long past, modern-day seers like Dan Quayle, and futurists who have yet to be born themselves, we proffer the following fearless forecast.

Rule number one: the traditional family will not go the way of the pet rock.

If this leaves you apoplectic, you're probably limiting your definition of just what a "traditional" family is. Those of us with rosy-hued slides of nuclear families and nuclear bomb shelters may forget that both tradition and the family unit are as fluid as a technicolor burp.

For instance, generations used to think nothing of living together under one roof. (Heck, sometimes they even took turns holding it up.) "Mixed" marriages and "blended" families were novel enough to buy TV executives yachts in the 1970s. And extended families are still the norm in homes around the world—together with unwashed dish sculptures, tantrums and "accidental" homicides.

Sure, more single parents, common law couples and childless marriages rear their heads each year. And there's the facile dirge about families dissolving in a sea of latchkeys, disarmed V-chips and bad luncheon meat. But we also have a poll suggesting that more than two out of three gentle Canucks believe that having one parent stay home is the best way to raise children. And a landmark national survey in the mid-1990s found that 83 per cent of Canadian children under 12 still live in families with two parents, the vast majority of them biological, rather than reconstructed by remarriage. The American figure is about 70 per cent. The British figure is more than 80 per cent. And the French figure could use the occasional shower between Bastille Days.

The inescapable fact is that the family will prevail, in whatever form it takes. We can clap a computer in our palm, but we still haven't found a better guest list for dinner. And the traditional method of making a family has not lost its pleasant side. Fundamentalists and family lawyers can relax.

Rule number two: science will confuse families even further.

The advent of genetic engineering hatches more medical, legal and moral issues than you can shake a test tube at. Debates over designer jeans, Adidas and spelling tests will graduate to litigation over designer genes, fetuses and DNA tests. Clever teenagers will mutate themselves and fight with their parents over the patent rights. Family films will score big laughs around the theme of "Send in the Clones." Bizarre biological sampling will create truly blended families, drawing from a gene pool so vast that they'll have to book Nuremberg Stadium for summer reunions. And in an age where legal academics pontificate over the potential liability of machines with artificial intelligence, "humanitarians" will zero in on robots' rights to family property.

Rule number three: the extended family will rise again.

You don't have to be a demographic doyen to divine that the baby boomer generation is on its way back to diapers, and fast. After monopolizing the media for years with everything from hula hoops and head shops to personal organizers and parental cop-outs like "quality time," everyone's favourite demographic bulge will inspire a brave new geriatric jamboree of demands and consumer products.

But when the witching hour comes, not all of them will be able to afford year-round golf, liposuction or a spectacular suicide leap into an active tropical volcano. At least some will move back in with the kids that they unleashed on the world. This is not a bad thing. Witness the Chinese proverb, "A family that has an old person in it possesses a jewel." Or the Serbian proverb, "Peaceful be the elderly, for they can no longer hear the shelling."

This will cultivate fertile ground for folks like estate planners, family counsellors and primal scream therapists. More families will look on a partly filled glass of water not as half-full or half-empty, but as a great place to park their elders' teeth. And just wait for the explosion in "seniors' lawyers" specializing in "living" wills (the dying kind being passé), hip replacement user agreements, and rocking chair accident litigation.

Rule number four: the family business will see a new heyday.

The family business is a huge part of our economy. A few years back, the Canadian Association of Family Enterprise declared that 45 per cent of our national Gross Domestic Product and 50 per cent of workers' pay cheques came from family businesses. The Mafia's figures are probably even higher.

This trend should continue, given the rise of home-based business and the fall of the downsizing axe in the merger-happy corporate world. Since these new entrepreneurs are likely to rope in close-knit associates, it follows that growing numbers of new businesses will be staffed by people swinging on the vines of a common family tree. Parents will hire their offspring, generating work experience, income-splitting and more heartache. And entrepreneurs will retain their own parents, giving the seniors yet another chance to build sweat equity. Employment standards and tax specialists will be busy.

Divorce lawyers will celebrate the added pressure on spouses who toil together. Mediators will book luxury cruises.

Rule number five: people will keep flogging the family.

The family will continue to be a lightning rod for statisticians, politicians, sociologists, lawyers and surreal TV sitcoms. We'll continue to regard the changing family portrait with caution (if not outright nausea), adjust the slant and dust it off once in awhile.

It's a brave new world out there for families. Even Dan Quayle would agree with the old Russian proverb, "As the family is, so is the offspring." Perhaps even the Russians would agree with the old Dan Quayle proverb, "The future will be better tomorrow."

Rules for choosing wedding ensembles

Source
Drusilya Popsokovich
Occupation
Red Alert Monitor, Russian Nuclear Substation No. III
Residence
Petropavlovsk-Kamtchatskiy, Russian Federation
Motto
"That was not my silo."

Rules

1 Respect everyone's feelings at this special time. But if people cannot agree, throw couple of switches and melt down hemisphere. Bickering should cease shortly.

2 Simple, matching white outfits will always be in fashion. But the reinforced lead lining, freeze-dried food pocket packets and emergency response transmitters may hinder fox-trotting at reception.

3 Do not forget to obtain appropriate permits. Be sure to bring extra roubles as "gratuity" for unpaid government workers minding desk.

4 Add extra touch of nostalgia and romance. Instead of usual corsages and boutonnieres, try red stars.

5 As you buy accessories, lock them securely, to discourage overzealous free market forces. Use elaborate system of pass-codes, with voice and fingerprint recognition, retinal verification, DNA sampling and above all else, abort button.

6 Remind both families that if they cannot put together their heads on some lousy little outfits, they will have terrible time living all together in some lousy little flat.

Father fodder

25

Pre-testing the paternal suitability of the dude in your household

Greetings and welcome to a "pop" quiz for new and expecting fathers. Test your knowledge of the sea of unwritten rules out there, and your ability to react to the following real-life scenarios. Bonus points will be awarded to anyone who thinks Lamaze is a hangout for Parisian laboratory rats.

1. Your wife (or significant other) interrupts a delightful Sunday afternoon round of Yahtzee to announce that she's expecting. Your immediate reaction is to:

   (a) casually inquire as to what she's expecting
   (b) deny responsibility and phone your travel agent about the next flight to Burkina Faso
   (c) buy shares in as many diaper companies as you can find
   (d) euphorically get on the phone and thank everyone from your great-uncle Floyd to the secretary-treasurer of your local hog marketing board.

2. It's the second month of the pregnancy, and it suddenly dawns on you that your better half is spending an unusual amount of time in

the part of the house where the chair flushes. Discuss the different avenues for expressing your concern, including the installation of runway-style night lights from the bedroom, and taking out a full-page ad in your local daily telling her you still love her.

3. It's your first prenatal class, you're shifting in your chair and your mind is on the Bahamas. From out of the blue, the instructor announces a surprise quiz and asks you to provide a complete description of the female reproductive system and how the body changes during pregnancy. Your reply is to:
   (a) hyperventilate and hope you wake up in an oxygen tent in some far-flung wing of the hospital
   (b) smile meekly and pretend you don't speak any English
   (c) discuss male anatomy and hope nobody notices the difference
   (d) instantly snap open your carefully tabbed copy of the leading text in the field and read the highlighted passages at length (together with your own insightful annotations) until everybody tells you to shut up already.

4. The four stages of labour are:
   (a) nausea, anxiety, cursing and relief
   (b) steady breathing, hurried breathing, rushed breathing and frenzied breathing
   (c) packing, driving to the hospital, parking the car and arguing with the cafeteria staff over their choice of the soup du jour

(d) collective bargaining, collective agreement, grievance and arbitration.

5. A sure sign that you are ready for that fateful trip to the hospital is when:
   (a) the water breaks
   (b) the front disc breaks
   (c) the whole car breaks
   (d) you just can't get any breaks.

6. Confounding the family pundits who have made small fortunes wagering on your queasiness in the past, you not only attend the birth, but capture the blessed event on home video. A good title for your production would be:
   (a) *The Good, the Bad and the Cuddly*
   (b) *All's Fair in Love and Wah*
   (c) *Diapers are a Girl's Best Friend*
   (d) *Womb with a View.*

7. When your brand new baby howls, a likely cause is:
   (a) the state of the Canadian dollar
   (b) the diet cola you fed him while your wife was out
   (c) that it's been three whole days since the latest Disney cartoon blockbuster, and you still haven't bought the corresponding linen, cup and teething ring
   (d) a full moon.

8. Briefly describe how you'd explain the fine art of diaper-changing to your colleague at the back of the morning bus, with nothing to demonstrate with except one of those little yellow, sticky things from the office. People are staring. You have 60 seconds.

9. Your four-week-old baby is the hit of your dinner party until she broadcasts a technicolor burp all over your boss's latest Ralph Lauren. Your next course of action is to:
   (a) follow Dr. Spock and attempt to reason with her (the baby, not your boss)
   (b) follow Mr. Spock and attempt to admonish the baby through a Vulcan mind-meld
   (c) follow the line to the nearest Canada Employment Centre
   (d) follow your conscience and do exactly what the baby did.

10. Heads up, one more to go. The best-selling tune of all time on the new parents' hit parade is:
   (a) *Lamazing Grace*
   (b) *Don't Worry Baby*
   (c) *The Times They are A-Changin'*
   (d) *Whatever Gets You Through the Night.*

Thank you for playing, and happy parenting.

Rules for picking up your kids from school

Source
Kivuku

Occupation
Tribal hunter

Residence
The Serengeti Plain, Tanzania

Motto
"An antelope a day keeps the medicine man away."

Rules

1 Approach the subjects slowly and carefully, remaining unseen until the last possible moment.

2 If you have anything sweet in your possession, seal it securely. The subjects have an uncanny sense of smell, and you may find yourself directly in the path of a stampeding herd.

3 Under no circumstances must you allow the subjects to amuse themselves with your spear, get greasy fingers in your headdress or use your shield as a toboggan.

4 If you encounter resistance, you may stun your quarry with a blowgun. Avoid poisons, except in the most dire of cases.

5 Once you have secured your prey, remove them to a shady spot and prepare them for the transport home. Strong burlap is recommended.

6 Respect the laws of nature. Only take what you need.

Eight great year-end gift ideas for teachers

27

A public service for harrassed parents

1

THE NEW AGE APPLE: organically grown, wax-free and hand-picked by legal migrant workers earning a fair wage

2

Handsome cotton-poly blend proclaiming, "My grade 10 class went to grade 11, and all I got was this lousy T-shirt"

3

Vanity licence plates bearing strong anti-homework slogans

4

Comprehensive legal opinion on the constitutionality of proposed changes to provincial school legislation (prepared by the student's solicitors)

5

Summer nostalgia: bubble bath that smells like a freshly washed school floor

6

Haunting poster (suitable for framing) reminding you that "The truth is out there"

7

Authentic-looking note on school board letterhead entitling teacher to bug out early on choice of three Friday afternoons

8

A timeless cult favourite: vanishing chalk

Rules for getting along in kindergarten

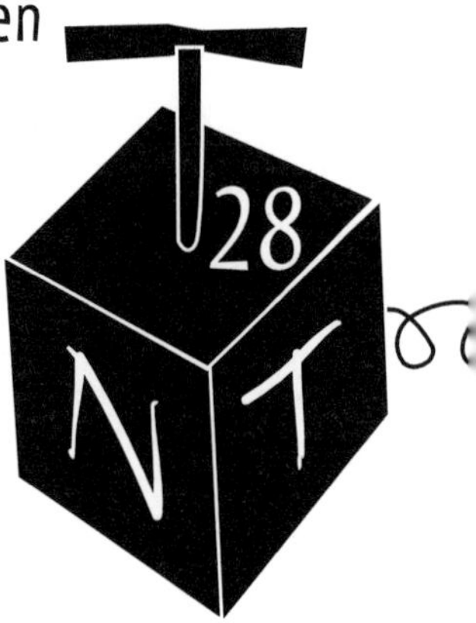

Sources
Shiresh Mettur/Bahrvalpur Kanji
Occupations
Carpenter/Railroad conductor
Residence
Krishnanagan, India/Gujranwala, Pakistan
Motto
"Death to the warmongering dogs!"/"A fiery hell to the imperialist jackals!"

Rules

1 Become more familiar with each other by starting off the year with a field trip to the nearest desert. Encourage interaction among the group by bringing only one canteen.

2 Exchange small, but lasting, gifts of friendship, such as cobras, scorpions and malaria.

3 Play a friendly game of "Whisper." (This is where you sit in a circle, whisper a sentence to the person next to you and see if you can recognize the sentence by the time the circle is complete.) But to ensure success and prevent any misunderstanding, shout in your neighbour's ear at the top of your lungs.

4 On homework sharing days, have your classmates play "Hot Potato" with live hand grenades.

5 On World Peace Day, divide into two teams and see who can stockpile the largest arsenal of sticks, stones and AK-47 assault rifles.

6 If all else fails, teach offensive classmates a real lesson with a small, peaceful, "defensive" nuclear explosion.

When we wished *être* was not to be

29

Pyrite memories of golden rules from French class

MISS BORKE WAS MY FRENCH TEACHER. And a formidable one she was, too. She would delight in striking dread in the drawers of every fourth grader in Wallace Wheatley Elementary School. She was swarthy. She wore dark, tinted glasses. And she was built like a fullback.

At the time, my sentence in her eerily tidy classroom teemed with the stresses of spelling bees and thousands of other ways to embarrass one's self before one's peers. But they seem positively carefree in today's world of nanoseconds, virtual reality and prepubescent career planning. Those were the days when the Quiet Revolution lived up to its name, computers were burly behemoths reserved for science fiction, and teaching aids in the schools didn't worry anyone.

There are two great rules that anyone grappling with French in the Canadian public school system quickly learns. The first is that nouns are either masculine (as in *le bar*) or feminine (as in *la crème de la crème*). The second, and by far the most important, is that the past tense of every verb is conjugated with the verb *avoir* (to have), except for 16 insidious aberrations, which require the verb *être* (to be).

To Miss Borke, these rules were as sacrosanct as anything could be. The sixth graders told us that they were chiselled into a blackboard by Commupwithes, the ancient Greek god of French, and handed down to Miss Borke on her first day of teaching many years ago, when our grandparents were in kindergarten.

With the first golden rule, we quickly learned that the best way to keep Miss Borke relatively safely at bay was to use nouns beginning with vowels whenever possible. This tactic allowed one to use *l'* without having to commit to *le* or *la*. The entire class took a vowel vow one frigid January morning during one of Miss Borke's rare sick days, which were greeted with the subdued sadness of a Stanley Cup parade.

We didn't actually *hate* Miss Borke. Lived in fear of her is closer to the mark.

She would work late into the night, sadistically plotting her merciless vocabulary quizzes, fixating on nouns beginning with consonants. We knew she did because she lived in the neighbourhood. Under cover of darkness, we'd sneak out of our homes, creep down the alley, huddle behind some prickly shrubs and watch. Watch the late-hour desk light in her clapboard duplex window, and shudder as her nicotine-soaked cackles wafted through the three small holes in her rotting window frame.

A couple of my classmates tried to beat her at her own game by making up nouns beginning with vowels just to avoid the burning *le/la* issue. Of course, she caught on each time, and rewarded their ingenuity with a week's detention—and the unspoken threat of The Strap. (Remember, these were the days before your average 10-year-old had a lawyer on retainer.)

With the second golden rule, Miss Borke made it her personal crusade to drill each of those infernal *être* verbs into our fragile, developing skulls.

She would periodically introduce the subject with the cunning of a stealth bomber and without warning, except an evil glint in her eye and a momentary grin, revealing a set of razor-sharp, brown-stained teeth. This lurid ritual reduced even the class bully, Bosco Neftin, to a quivering mass of denim, to say nothing of what it did to the bed-wetters.

The drama would unfold as she picked on four luckless souls to regurgitate four *être* verbs each. If your brain miraculously did not turn to Silly Putty and you spit out four, she would grunt and shuffle down the aisle of shaking desks to descend on her next victim.

Three correct responses meant a black mark next to your name in her book.

In the more likely event that you only got one or two, she would hover over your desk like a crane with a dangling wrecking ball, and pulverize you with a stare unfit for non-military use.

If you blanked out totally, you won an all-expenses-paid trip to the staff room sink for a week. Nothing is more devastating to a peer-conscious gaggle of kids than a case of dishpan hands.

As I go about my daily business in what passes for the adult world, I sometimes slide my rose-coloured glasses past my greying temples and remember Miss Borke, a huge potful of years and miles away.

To this day, I can hear her flat, mechanical drone— "These are the 16 *être* verbs. *Know* them!"—and it still causes a ripple in my belly.

In my darkest dreams, I am walking down a supermarket aisle with my kids, and one of them pulls a Froot Loops box from the shelf, revealing an unmistakably evil eye and brown teeth lurking carnivorously behind it. I dredge up about half of the 16 *être* verbs, and then go numb. My son and daughter gaze up at me in horror. Other shoppers frown in my general direction. Stock boys less than half my age turn away and shake their heads sadly.

I resolve to spend my next lunch hour in the library, double-checking a French language primer—just in case. Now that's what I call a *real* lesson learned.

DROP AND GIVE ME SIXTEEN!
Aller... Venir... Tomber... monter... Descendre...
GASP

Rules for attending school reunions

Source

Nehemiah "Sign Here" Rubinfield

Occupation

Film producer

Residence

Los Angeles, California

Motto

"If you're not at the table, bubba, you're on the menu."

Rules

1. Top-notch prep counts big-time, babe. So your first stops are makeup, wardrobe and dialogue-coaching.
2. It's okay to have your fitness trainer move in with you for up to six months before the big gig. But have them sign a release of any palimony claims. No exceptions.
3. When you get to the reunion, help yourself to extra blank name tags, to list your latest box office credits.
4. If you forget a face, never let on. They may be The Next Big Thing. If you're cornered on this, tell them you're in therapy and you haven't worked up to your school years yet.
5. Beware of wannabes who can do diddly for your resumé. You know, the dorks that are asked who they are, and answer with only their name.
6. Life's too short for aimless small talk, babe. Be up front about your hair implants, your fishnet stockings and your foot fetish. And tell them you're okay with that.

The Craven

31

A Poe-etic,
recurring nightmare
of inadequate
preparation

ONCE UPON A CLASSROOM CRISIS, with guts locked in cold steel vises,
Sat I with my cohorts, cut to slices, behind closed exam room door;
When suddenly my heart fluttered, a meek murmur uttered;
I could ace this test, I muttered, or at least get a passing score;
Put down the right answers, and pretend it was all a bore—
Save my butt, and nothing more.

Tremblingly did I tarry that dark, frozen February
As many wary students had thus sealed their fate before;
Petrified, I sat and listened, shuddered as my temples glistened,
Transfixed was my good eye positioned, glancing at the door;
To escape with my grades intact, and my future secure—
Wishing that, and nothing more.

As the system I silently dissed, face in a hideous twist,
Our names they read from a list, and our best efforts implored;
Squirming to stay stable, I gripped my rotting table,
As if in some macabre fable, a nightmare to explore;
Tearfully tearing open the test booklet du jour—
Bracing myself, and nothing more.

Trembling insanely at what the devils asked so vainly,
For the answers very plainly had no relevance whatso'er;
My being now shaking, skin crawling, palpitating,
I felt all my being hating this turgid tug-of-war,
The merciless, endless thrusts from my edu-matador—
Drawing blood, and nothing more.

Deep into my soul cloaking, long sat I there, pondering, choking
Terror's restless smoking my tell-tale heart could not ignore;
Through frenzied prayers unspoken, I sought a heavenly token
That my memory block would be broken, as in years of yore;
This I callowly craved as the clock closed in for the gore—
Minutes to go, and nothing more.

"Villains!" I screeched, the solemn stillness now breached,
My G.P.A., I beseeched, they quit cutting down to the core;
But their questions ever pointing, my epitaph anointing,
At my career gun-pointing, bashed me with a two-by-four;
Ushering my fall to a pit of pendulum-pocked carnivores—
Struck me dumb, and nothing more.

And those demon questions, so daunting, remain wanting, ever haunting,
My tortured conscience taunting, as I wither on the classroom floor;
The exam's end encroaching, others' expectant sighs approaching,
In defiance of my reproaching, the bell tolls and others outpour,
And those questions, aimed at sending me to Hades' deathly shore,
I can't answer, Quoth the Craven—"Pass nevermore!"

Rules for getting laughs from a tough audience

Source
Chuan Chai Ti

Occupation
Monk

Residence
Dagla Gompo, Tibet, China

Motto
"Listen to your hair growing."

Rules

1 Meditate intently on the essence of the banana peel and its place in the order of nature before you would contrive to slip on it onstage.

2 Be mindful of the five elements representing both the proper functioning of the internal organs, and the psychological health, of club comedy: torturous relationships, the "F" word, assorted bodily functions and fluids, Jack Nicholson impressions and draft beer. Departing from these avenues is a sign of self-preoccupation, and a betrayal of the vow to kowtow to the Tao.

3 Where there is disharmony between your words and the silence of the audience, remind them that, like the snake and the crane, the struggle is necessary to our journey of matter, life and consciousness. If that does not amuse them, accept their energetically bestowed gifts of tomatoes with humility and grace.

4 What is most essential to nurturing life is refining the body. As the incorporeal soul resides in the liver, invite them to raise their spirits with goat brandy.

5 Your every breath, word or nuance can lead to great fortune or untold calamity. Deliver each punchline as if it was your last—though in some cases, this can become self-fulfilling.

6 When you find yourself dying, bury the house microphone in the nearest potted plant. The device will assume your shape, freeing your life force to ascend to a higher spiritual plane. If your plane is late, seek a voucher—or at least an extra moist towelette.

Standing up at comedy college

33

Memoirs of learning the laws of making funny

I BELIEVE THAT AT SOME POINT, each of us gets one cosmic, pivotal message. It could be anything from a sign from God to that million-dollar envelope from Ed McMahon. Mine comes in a terse newspaper clip in the spring of 1997, heralding an unprecedented, week-long course in comedy at Toronto's Humber College that August.

Sure, I always wanted to be a comedian, to which years of amateur performances attest. And I did leave an underworked and overpaid legal career to start a business, which includes writing and performing my idea of comedy at conferences and special events. But the prospect of formal training in comedy strikes me as orgiastic, to say nothing of what it would do for my agent—or better yet, decent clients whose money I've taken for the privilege over the years.

The organizers impress: Humber's Joe Kertes, whose novel, *Winter Tulips,* sprouted a Leacock Medal for Humour, and Mark Breslin, impresario of the Yuk-Yuk's Komedy Kabaret chain, who built his success on laughs, if not spelling. Instructors include Joe Flaherty, dean of the classic *SCTV* series, and like luminaries leading lectures, panels and workshops on stand-up, sketch, screenwriting and more.

"We can't make you funny," they boom, "but we can make you funnier if you are." Convinced that looks aren't everything, I get their brochure, dip into my formerly sacred quarterly tax installment fund for the fee, and dispatch the required writing sample and work-in-progress. Though I've been writing and performing comedy for years, this is only my second attempt at pure stand-up—a monologue without the safety net of a specific audience in mind. I come up with 15 minutes on the end of the world. ("The Parti Quebecois will insist on Quebec's inalienable right to blow up *separately* from the rest of Canada…")

Remarkably, they accept my application. As I explain the reason for my upcoming absence to my kids, I wonder whether I'm getting too old for this. After all, isn't the prototypical junior comedian a gangly, pimply undergrad with an attitude, a preference for stimulants and a room in mommy's basement?

As it turns out, my 100-odd classmates are a mishmash of hairlines, colours and hygienic standards. They range from a former courier for the Sandinistas and a masseuse who once filched Eric Burden's shoe to a retired Federal Court judge and a pun-prone Wal-Mart greeter. (As proof that comedy imitates life, the sole New Yorker is expelled on day one for a bad attitude.) There are professional comics looking to improve their craft, novices craving a new career and grandfathers wanting to have some fun for a change. Not a toastmaster in sight.

Although we are as diverse as the leftovers at a Yugoslavian revival buffet, we discover a fundamental, shared bond that seems to motivate those who defy humanity's second-greatest fear after dying (speaking in public). The bond is neurosis. Of course, dying has a featured role in comedy, too: if you don't get a laugh after 15 seconds onstage, you are considered luncheon meat.

A CBC TV crew joins us for the week, intent on immortalizing the proceedings for an upcoming edition of *Adrienne Clarkson Presents.* As further proof that comedy imitates life, many of us largely ignore the camera, just as many Canadians largely ignore the CBC.

The call to arms begins with *Laugh-In* creator George Schlatter, a gracious and gregarious comedy giant, who challenges us to break free of the insipid, homogenized pulp propagated on today's TV sitcoms, and to take a risk. This from the man who persevered through eight takes to coax President Nixon to say "Sock it to me" on the air.

My actual workshop begins badly. A dozen of us await our instructor, whom, we're told, is careening to campus in a cab from the airport. Since it's a stand-up workshop, we refuse to take this sitting down. (But being Canadian, we do anyway.) Sweeping in outrageously late, clad in black from braless halter top to leather pants and platform clogs, is the founder of LA's daring "Uncabaret." Her mission: "alternative" comedy, a freestyle, arty backlash against the hackneyed, generic approach to club stand-up propagated on nightly television.

Our next shock comes when she asks if we're ready for the workshop on alternative comedy. We tell her no, we signed up for the regular stand-up class. Okay, she chirps.

But is it really? As we recite our raw works in progress, she confesses that she has not perused our precious pearls. She pushes us to see the comedy in our own lives, rather than parrot pre-scripted, impersonal observations that drop an anvil on the emotional bond which successful comedians form with their audiences.

All of this, of course, is as foreign to my literal approach as her wardrobe is to a Greek Orthodox funeral.

We learn that written perfection never happens verbally, where interacting with the audience becomes the performance. So the idea is to "get off the page and onto the stage" by shifting our focus from specific words to characters and emotions. I begin to believe this after the largest laughs during our initial read-throughs come from ad libs. (Try this. It works.)

But I relapse, clinging to the shattered shards of my rosary of one-liners. Why, I wonder, would anyone care about my experiences or emotions? She exults that the real point of stand-up is sharing human experience and bonding—not just getting laughs—and that any comedian who truly believes that her life is not worth presenting onstage had better get a new life. We gulp audibly.

Although we learn that success in comedy requires a measure of cockiness and guts, we get a reality check when a 22-year Hollywood screenwriter is asked what it takes to succeed. In reply, he grabs the collar of his co-panellist, the vice-president of programming for Canada's new Comedy Channel, and tearfully pleads, "Oh, *please!*"

In our scant free time—red-eyed late or bleary-eyed early—we write the monologues which we're expected to perform at the students' show on our final night, Black Friday. Between sessions, I practice my routine in enough men's rooms to wonder whether I'll be able to go onstage without the reassuring echo of an automatic urinal flush.

One instructor, a writer on *Saturday Night Live* during its funny years and the first female editor of *National Lampoon,* sums up the industry's ethics by noting that while you can catch more flies with honey, it works even better with dead meat. As she prefaces her autograph in my notebook with the words, "I'll never forget last night," I'm reminded that the showbiz morals which she gleefully skewers are as sturdy as my five-year-old's baby teeth.

Populating a provocative panel on the state of comedy is Hart Pomerantz, the irreverent, wisecracking lawyer on CBC's old *This is the Law* series and the creator of two others, which he swears were cancelled due to *high* ratings. He laments three barriers to successful careers in comedy: the lack of supporting infrastructure in Canada ("Comedy is not a profession, but an illness"); Canadians' reluctance to criticize, a key element of comedy; and increasing social permissiveness, which denudes comic possibilities because comedy depends on subversion and the subconscious.

I ask Joe Flaherty about *SCTV*'s jaunt in Edmonton 15 years earlier, a period in which he acknowledges that the show hit its creative peak. He responds with a rant against a local newspaper editorial celebrating the troup's departure, then accuses me of writing it.

By the time Black Friday arrives, we're approaching mirth meltdown. Our show will feature two and a half hours of sketch and stand-up comedy. Three people in my group chicken out. A fourth soldier, my buddy from BC, leaves the building just moments before his cue. And why not? The auditorium and stage are large, the lights are blinding and the CBC cameras are rolling.

I decide not to let the audience off that easily, and regale them about my escape from the practice of law ("I am a refugee from a cult…") and scenes from a first-generation Canadian's childhood ("The other kids wore tie-dye. I wore haunting grey and brown cast-offs from Hungarian State Garment Collective Number 51…"). Through the blinding stage lights ripples more laughter and applause than I deserve. When Joe Flaherty offers kind words, I contemplate walking on water, but settle for gulping a glass of it instead. Maybe there's something to this alternative comedy stuff after all.

At the closing banquet, we hear the legendary Steve Allen, whose credits include founding the talk show as the first host of the *Tonight Show;* creating other great TV series; composing a world-record 3,500 songs; writing 49 books; and lecturing in philosophy, "to name just two," as his warm-up act, Dave Broadfoot, points out.

Mr. Allen declares that the main thing sustaining his career for 50 years is that he hasn't died yet. He sees life as one glorious straight line, and encourages us to realize in what regard it's outrageous and to communicate that. When asked what the future of comedy is, he replies that the future is whatever is going to happen. It is like an audience with the Pope.

I feel exhilarated, liberated and saturated. Flying home to the prairies, I contemplate the shock of shifting from 16 hours of comedy per day back to the real world.

I needn't have worried. Awaiting me in the airport crowd is my family, all sporting outrageously loud ties and the classic nose-and-glasses. Everyone laughs. Nobody gets arrested.

Mindful of my new creed that a full existence is the best preparation for any performer, I resolve to live a life that's both useful and worth putting onstage. And *that,* as Lily Tomlin used to say, is the truth.

Rules for using public washrooms

Source
Taddeuz "Skins" Czawkorzjewicz

Occupation
Drummer, "Brachtwurst Benders" bar band

Residence
Monchengladbach, Germany

Motto
"All I want to do is dance, Herr Major."

Rules

1 During lineups, pull out two spoons and play *Taps.*

2 If you practise your conducting, face *away* from the pissoiren.

3 Understand our collective impermanence. When jotting great thoughts on the walls, please limit your medium to washable crayon.

4 If vandals leave the taps running, mop up the floor with them.

5 Celebrate the source of all life. Hum the *Blue Danube Waltz* with every flush.

6 Never abandon your humanity. Look people in the eye when you converse. If this upsets them, stop peeking under the door of their stall and wait for them to come out.

The strange case of the distraining Iranian

35

Featuring film noir-style tax battle-axe, "Ace" Malone

IT WAS ANOTHER LATE NIGHT AT THE OFFICE. I had just returned from the men's room with the latest issue of the *Value Added Tax Tribunal Reports* when my phone rang.

"Ace Malone here."

"Congratulations, Mr. Malone. I represent Teddy's Tidy Tuna-on-a-Stick Company, and you have been selected at random to receive a free demonstration of our new line of—"

There was something fishy about the caller, but I didn't let on. I put him on hold and contacted my pal, "Buzz" Grabarkewitz, who worked the night shift at the Corporations Branch. Just as I suspected all along. The telephone solicitation was not authorized by the company's articles of incorporation. I notified the proper authorities, hung up on the caller and went back to work.

I smiled at Bertha, my 44-calibre Income Tax Act, which I kept in a snub-nosed holster slung over my coat rack. Big Bertie and I had been through a lot together. Life with her has been a lot easier since they knocked her down to 800 pages and nixed the regs.

I cut my teeth on the Phlegm Bungalow Merger and a string of tax appeals that would freeze your assets. I cut my opponents down to size with a volley of arguments that leave their cases full of holes. I cut myself shaving last week.

I'd been working on a major corporate lease for my favourite client, Rocco "The Big Cheese" Smith. The whole East Side knew that The Big Cheese was up to his buns in debts. His holding company was low on lettuce and his top eggs could no longer cut the mustard. Because he was in a real pickle, I relished the challenge, and managed to sandwich it in between a Butter Business Bureau claim and a Mayo Clinic audit spread across my desk.

I was about to dig into it when it happened. My door flew open, and in burst four tough-looking mugs in black trench coats over three-piece, pinstriped suits, with Perrier bottles dangling out of the corners of their mouths.

"You Malone?" gurgled the bubbly one.

"Sorry, boys. You'll have to make an appointment with my secretary." I decided to play it coy. "Now if you'll run along, I have some serious work to do."

"You're cute, Malone. Real cute." The foreman pointed to an impeccably clad figure entering the room behind him. "Do you have any idea who this is?"

"Allen Funt?" I played for time. There was always the chance that I could hit them up for a fancy hourly consulting fee.

"Wrong, floating charge debenture breath. It's Dahkk Sader, the famous West Side solicitor, late of the Iranian bar."

It was Dahkk Sader, all right. He'd been getting a lot of bad ink on account of his rolling over when the feds questioned his recent transfer of shares. Then there was the even more taxing matter of his daughter's rejecting the advances of the heir to an American beer conglomerate. She told the *Clarion* that she'd never go through life as Sader-Budweiser.

"So it is. What's up, Dahkk?"

He sat down after one of his patsies cleared a pile of files off one of my chairs with his left shoe. "Mr. Malone, can I trust you?"

"It depends. Is this a social call or is Judge Frump on one of her search and seize kicks again?" I glanced over at Bertha on the other end of my office, then back to Sader's party, all of whom had their hands in their pockets and pointed in my direction.

"You had better be careful, Mr. Malone. My articling students all have the latest, most deadly Income Tax Act. Fully annotated." He lit a cigar and the room was suddenly overcome by the smell of burning Double Bubble.

"Don't be silly, Sader. You know better than to use those big books on me in here. The whole neighbourhood would hear them go off. Besides, you'd blow your covers."

He replied by pointing to his most earnest-looking student, a redwood-sized redhead. "Ah, but Biff here has the unannotated pocket version. No one would ever notice..."

He had a point. I graciously informed him that I would waive my customary consulting fee if they promised not to ransack the office. I'd gone through my sixth Scandinavian janitor that month and didn't want to scare off number seven.

So I dummied up and got an earful of Sader's story. He was up the creek all right. Seems like he was caught with his hand in the cookie jar again. Only this time his mother was pressing charges, as the goods were baked especially for her Kiwanis luncheon that Thursday. He had wanted the jar seized for non-payment of rent. The law calls this "distraining." I call it "distracting."

He had one of his stooges feather-dust the top of my desk before setting his genuine patent hyena-skin satchel on it. He ordered Biff to dynamite the lock with a firecracker, claiming to have forgotten the combination. Then he pulled out a thick, maroon envelope.

"So, Mr. Malone. You will take the case?"

"Naw. It's second-hand. Besides, the lock is in a thousand pieces. You'd be in breach of the implied warranty of merchantable quality under the Sale of Goods Act if you let me have it."

"Not the satchel, you idiot. *My* case!"

"Oh." I had to think fast. "Well, I'm afraid I can't. If memory serves, I once acted for your mother's next-door neighbour's cousin in a reverse takeover bid, so there would seem to be a conflict of interest."

"A conflict of interest? *What* conflict of interest?"

"Well, I figured that if you were dumb enough not to plug me after that "What's up, Dahkk" line, you'd be dumb enough to fall for anything."

"You leave me no choice, Mr. Malone." He closed what was left of his briefcase and popped eight boysenberry jujubes in one motion. "We have Edna."

Damn. He knew he had me. Edna was my lucky racquet. I must have left her at the club after thrashing Black Bart Brannigan last week. Sader knew that a stiff couldn't last five minutes in this business without good squash equipment.

"You win. Where's my retainer?"

To make a long story short, I got Sader off the hook by trying to convince the court of the irreparable harm that would befall the law of corporate securities if Her Honour convicted my client of theft of a cookie. The judge bought it.

Unfortunately, so did my client, just four days after the trial. They found his satchel floating in the river along with a dog-eared copy of the classic tax treatise, *Deductive Reasoning Made E-Z.* Evidently, one of his more disgruntled associates had elected to cement their relationship.

As for yours truly, I've been doing some serious thinking about eighty-sixing the corporate tax biz. Too big a strain on the old ticker.

The wife says I should settle down to a more peaceful way of making a sawbuck, like maybe some mercenary work in Kosovo, or teaching Bhuddist semantics in an inner-city junior high school. As they say at the meat market, you never know when your number's up.

I was walking home late the other night when a punk came up to me.

He said, "Got a light, bud?"

I said, "No, but there's a Diet Fresca machine across the street. Tell 'em Jack Malone sent you."

"Jack?" he squawked. "Hey, I thought your monicker was Ace Malone."

"It used to be, but I was nonsuited last week, so I demoted myself."

"I gotta hand it to you, Malone," he snapped.

"Yeah," I drawled, poker-faced. "I'm a real card."

Rules for dancing with lawyers

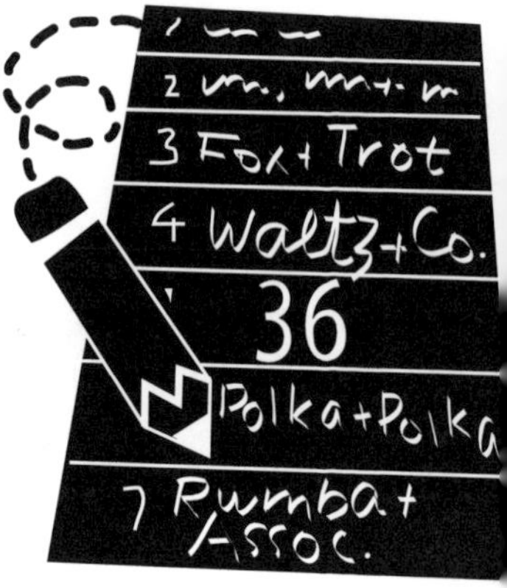

Source
Fado Saudade

Occupation
Football club administrator

Residence
Passo Fundo, Brazil

Motto
"Football is no mere matter of life or death."

Rules

1 Introduce yourself to your legal advocates in the universal language of humankind. Kick a football at their skull and find out whether they can do a header.

2 Discuss fees at the first interview. If they will not accept payment in football trading cards, coffee beans or old bossa nova records, express indignation and threaten to take your complaint to the international human rights tribunal.

3 Have them assess the merits of your case. If they feel that it could go either way in court, ask whether the matter could be resolved by a shootout.

4 Determine the true costs of losing your case, i.e. whether your compatriots would parade you through the streets in disgrace, torch 20 hectares of rainforest in your name and then send your photo to Greenpeace.

5 Insist on proper decorum throughout the proceedings. If your lawyer receives a red card in court, ask for the opportunity to field a substitute.

6 If you win the case, hug your legal representatives, race around the courtroom, wave your flag in the air, weep openly and exchange shirts with your opponents.

Singin' in the court

37

A criminal play in three-quarter time starring a boy, a beanstalk and a giant pain

Cast

THE JUDGE, a cranky old coot with a deep baritone
CLERKS #1 AND #2, who always wanted to be the Supremes
CROWN PROSECUTOR, who strives to perform with conviction
DEFENCE COUNSEL, who rarely sits on defence on any point
J. G. GIANT, a gentle, if not somewhat bewildered, victim of a *major* growth disorder
JACK VAN DER BEANSTALK, an irreverent little troublemaker
THE JURY, being 12 able-bodied, but not necessarily angry, people

Act I

(Enter CLERKS #1 and #2 from upstage. They march to, and stand behind, their respective desks in the left and right foreground, below the elevated bench, Clerk #1 to the audience's left and Clerk #2 to the audience's right.)

(Enter CROWN, who marches to, and stands behind, the prosecutor's table to the audience's left.)

(Enter DEFENCE and JACK. Defence marches to defence counsel's table to the audience's right and stands behind it. Jack saunters behind him, smiling and waving to the audience. When he reaches the table, he pulls out one of two chairs there, and plops down. When Defence kicks the chair discreetly, Jack jumps up to attention.)

(Enter JURY. They take their seats in the jury box.)

(Enter JUDGE, who moves to his place of honour behind the bench.)

MUSIC: *Symphony No. 5* by Ludwig van Beethoven

CLERKS

Order in court!
Order in court!

(Judge takes a seat and nods at Jury, Crown, Defence and audience. Clerks, Crown and Defence sit down. Eventually, Jack catches on and drops to his seat.)

MUSIC: *Blue Danube Waltz* by Johann Strauss

JUDGE

Welcome to the court.

CLERKS

The court, the court.

JUDGE

Law is a great sport.

CLERKS

Great sport, great sport.

JUDGE

We will have a trial…

CLERKS

A trial, a trial…

JUDGE

In song with a smile.

CLERKS

A smile, a smile.

JUDGE

Young Jack is accused…

CLERKS

Accused, accused…

JUDGE
Of stealing a goose…

CLERK
A goose, a goose…

JUDGE
And some gold coins,
oh what loot,
And a golden harp to boot.

CROWN
And the Crown will move
To attempt to prove
That Jack's guilty
That he's guilty.

DEFENCE
The defence will go
And proceed to show
That Jack's innocent
As the clean, pure,
white, driven snow.

JUDGE
Each side will call its case;
The Giant will show his face;
Then Jack will take his place;
And we'll sort it all out
with elegance and grace.

MUSIC: *Symphony No. 5* by Ludwig van Beethoven

CLERKS
Start with the Crown!
Start with the Crown!

MUSIC: *Old Macdonald Had A Farm*

CROWN
The Crown calls J.G. Giant.

CLERKS
E-I-E-I-O.

(Enter GIANT, who stomps to the witness stand, near Clerk #2.)

MUSIC: T*he Farmer in the Dell*

CLERKS
The witness take the stand,
The witness take the stand,
Hope like heck you tell the
truth,
The witness take the stand.

MUSIC: *Clementine*

CROWN
Mr. Giant, what's your
full name?

GIANT
Jolly Green and I'm proud.

CROWN
Can you tell the Court what
happened
At your castle in the clouds?

GIANT
[verse 2]
I was rolling all my
gold coins,
Month-end accounting,
I speak;
I'm adding a decimal point
When in walks
that young pipsqueak.

(He indicates Jack.)

CROWN
[verse 3]
Let the record show
he pointed
At the accused, namely Jack.
Tell us in words
not disjointed
What happened there
after that.

MUSIC: *My Bonnie*

GIANT
I yelled "FEE-FI-FO-FUM!"
and chased him,
He grabbed a bag of gold
in flight,
He started to tickle
my left foot
And then he tickled
at my right.
[verse 2]
I am quite ticklish, I admit it,
Falling to the floor,
laughing, I'm.

CROWN
And at the end of your
laughing fit,
What did you tell Jack at that
time?

GIANT
I said, "Bring back,
bring back,
"Oh, bring back my
gold coins to me, to me.
"Say, Jack, say, Jack,
"Oh, bring back my
gold coins to me."

MUSIC: *Oh, Susannah*
by Stephen Foster

CROWN
So Jack took the bag of
gold coins
And then ran away, did he?

GIANT
Yes, he ran out to my garden,
Climbed down a huge
beanstalk tree.
[chorus]
Oh, that rotter,
stole my bag of gold,
So I come to this
ol' court house
So my story can be told.
[verse 2]
Late next day he showed
his face
In my castle once more;
I was strumming
on my golden harp,
I didn't know the score.
[chorus]
Oh, that robber, my lunge
did he duck,
Tickled me once more,
then snatched my harp,
Oh, what confounded pluck!

CROWN
[verse 3]
Did it bother you,
the missing harp?

GIANT
It really strung me out.

CROWN
Did you give him any
words so sharp?

GIANT
I did "FEE-FI-FO-FUM"
shout.
[verse 4]
I ran right outside after him,
He climbed down that
beanstalk.
He flashed me a big,
goofy grin,
Back home I had to walk.
Oh, that rascal, stole
my gold harp, too,
And I come to this
ol' courthouse so that
he can get his due.

CROWN
[verse 5]
Good Giant, please don't you
go balk,

There is something
I can't place:
When Jack climbed down
the beanstalk,
How come you did not
give chase?

GIANT

[verse 6]
Well, I'll tell you all a secret
For which my pride
really stings:
I try not to climb beanstalks,
I'm afraid of the
darned things.
[chorus]
Oh, that blighter, stole
my harp and coins.
Makes me madder
than a hatter
And brings on hives
in my loins.

CROWN

[verse 7]
Did you see Jack again
after that?

GIANT

You're darned right,
now hear this:
The next day on a couch I sat
With my fav'rite pet, Alice.
[verse 8]
Now Alice is a magic goose,
She lays pure golden eggs;
I'd say, "Honk if you
like pizza,"
She would sit right up
and beg.
[verse 9]
So Jack stomped through
my parlour door,
He tickled through my shoes,
I fell down laughing
on the floor
And he grabbed
my golden goose.
[chorus]
Oh, that wiener,
stole my goose, Alice,
So I come to this
ol' courthouse
Without absence of malice.

MUSIC: *Beautiful Dreamer* by Stephen Foster

CROWN

So Mr. Giant, what happened
then?

GIANT

He escaped down that
big beanstalk again.

CROWN
Did you follow him? What
did you do?

GIANT
I had to follow, he took Alice,
too!
I closed my eyes and
started to climb
Down through the clouds
and air pollution grime.
Looking down thousands
of feet below,
I almost threw up,
I got vertigo (wah-oo).

CROWN
Then what happened, tell us
please, spare no woe.

GIANT
[verse 2]
About halfway down,
felt something rock;
Jack was chopping down the
whole darn beanstalk.
Soon I was falling at
breakneck speed;
A soft landing was just
what I would need.
Wanted a mattress,
feathered and flat;
Got a cabbage patch,
landed with a splat!

CROWN
When did you call the police
'bout Jack?

GIANT
Right after I washed
the squash off my slacks
(wah-oo);
He took my gold and
gave me a bad back.

MUSIC: *Symphony No. 5* by Ludwig van Beethoven

CROWN
No more questions.
It's your witness.

(Crown sits down. Defence stands up.)

MUSIC: *Alouette*

DEFENCE
Mr. Giant, had you
met my client
Before his three trips
to your castle?

GIANT
I never saw him before
He showed his mug
at my door.

DEFENCE
Are you sure?

GIANT
Evermore,
Oh-oh-oh-oh…

DEFENCE
So you've cited,
could you have invited
Jack to visit your place
and forgot?

GIANT
Invited him and forgot?
No way, absolutely not.

DEFENCE
Sales Jack sought?

GIANT
Not this plot.

DEFENCE
Took a shot. (shrugs)

GIANT
Oh, what rot.
Ho-ho-ho-ho…

DEFENCE
So you have told you own
the bag of gold,
The golden harp and
the gold goose, too.

GIANT
I surely, most truly do
As sure as I sing to you.

DEFENCE
So it's true?

GIANT
Yes, boo-hoo.

DEFENCE
Were they new?

GIANT
Residue.

DEFENCE
Déjà vu?

GIANT
Peekaboo.

(Giant waves to the goose.)

Boo-hoo-boo-hoo…

DEFENCE
Could you've striven, say,
to have a-given

All that gold to Jack
as a present?

GIANT
Not a hope in Hades, no;
Never met the little schmo.

DEFENCE
Even so—

GIANT
He's John Doe.

DEFENCE
On you grow?

GIANT
He's my foe.

DEFENCE
Quid pro quo?

GIANT
No bon mots.

DEFENCE
Finito.

GIANT
Cheerio.

(Giant steps down and returns to the audience. Defence sits down, takes a long swig of something to drink, hiccups loudly, and dabs at his perspiring face. Crown rises.)

CROWN
Oh-oh-oh-oh,
So we now face the end of
the Crown's case.

JUDGE
So be it, hence, we'll hear
the Defence.

Act II

(Defence rises.)

MUSIC: *Old MacDonald Had a Farm*

DEFENCE
The Defence calls the
accused.

CLERKS
E-I-E-I-O.

MUSIC: *The Farmer in the Dell*

The witness take the stand,
The witness take the stand,
Hope like heck you tell
the truth,
The witness take the stand.

MUSIC: *Daisy, Daisy*

DEFENCE
Jackie, Jackie, Crown's case
has been professed,
So tell us how you got
into this mess.

JACK
Well, the whole thing
got started
When my ma said,
half-hearted,
"Go out now and sell the cow
"So we can buy some food
processed."
[verse 2]
So I left home,
with old Bossy in tow.
I ran into some guy
I didn't know.
He started to me a-talking,
"No need for further
walking,"
He said, "How do, give me
Miss Moo
"For some magic beans
that will grow."

MUSIC: *Yankee Doodle*

JACK
Then I took the beans
on home
And showed them to
my old ma;
She threw them out
the window
And shouted, "What
bologna!"
Sent me to bed with no meal,
No goodnight kiss puckered.
It sure looked like a bad deal
And like I had been
suckered.
[verse 2]
Next day I got up for school
And jeepers, beg your
pardon,
Saw a giant beanstalk (cool!)
Growing huge in our garden.
Put my books down,
got a rope,
Started climbing the stalk;
Maybe, maybe was my hope,
This was not another crock.

MUSIC: *I've Been Working on the Railroad*

DEFENCE
What did you think you
would find there?

JACK
Really couldn't say.

DEFENCE
Didn't you know enough
to beware
Of the Giant's entranceway?

JACK
Heck, no, I thought that
the bean man
Had it all worked out
with him.
I thought I just could
march in and
Help myself with vim.

DEFENCE
Were you hassled when
In the castle glen
You met Mr. Giant?

JACK
Guess it's hard to say,
He wanted to play,
He seemed defiant.
I saw him in the kitchen
with gold bags;
He seemed very rich and
I thought
He wouldn't be missin'
a small swag,
So I tickled him a lot.

[verse 2]
Then I grabbed a bag
of fine gold,
Ran back down the stalk.

DEFENCE
Did the Giant leave
his household?

JACK
He ran at me down his walk;
I thought it was just for fun,
so
Waved goodbye and yelled,
"See you soon!"
He never followed me down,
though.
Ma loved those doubloons.

DEFENCE
So what happened then?
Did you go again?

JACK
Darn tootin', I wanted more.
Tickled his foot sharp,
Grabbed his big gold harp,
Left him laughing on the
floor.

DEFENCE
Did he come running in
pursuit?

JACK
Sure he did, just like the last
time.

DEFENCE
Did he follow you down the
bean shoot?

JACK
No, it was an easy climb.

MUSIC: *This Old Man*

DEFENCE
So then, Jack, you went back?

JACK
Sure I did, I ain't no quack;
Climbed the beanstalk,
didn't balk,
Had nothing to lose;
Saw the Giant's golden goose.

DEFENCE
[verse 2]
Did the Giant seem
quite cross?

JACK
He told me to go get lost,
But a koochie-koochie-koo
Through his big old shoe
Made him smile once more
on cue.

[verse 3]
Grabbed the goose and
some eggs,
Left him all of the fowl dregs,
Put the bird smack
in my sack,
Gave him a grin fine,
Ran down my favourite vine.

MUSIC: *Pop Goes the Weasel*

DEFENCE
Did the Giant follow you
down
The beanstalk that occasion?

JACK
Yes, he did, he had on
a frown
Just for persuasion.

DEFENCE
Was he following in
your tracks?
Did you hear your knees
knock?

JACK
Yes, yes, but I found an axe…
Chop! went the beanstalk!

MUSIC: *Symphony No. 5* by Ludwig van Beethoven

DEFENCE

No more questions.
Over to you.

(Defence sits down. Crown rises.)

MUSIC: *Home on the Range*

CROWN

So tell us, in chant when you
met the Giant
Didn't you notice his
angry glare?

JACK

Well, I sure could see
he was crazy 'bout me;
We played tag each time I
was there.

CROWN

Jack, could you not see
That taking the gold
was robbery?

JACK

No way, that's no line, all of
that gold was mine,
The bean man had promised
it to me.

MUSIC: *Michael, Row the Boat Ashore*

CROWN

Did he promise you
gold coins,
Harp and goose, huh?

JACK

No, those words were
not employed,
Never used 'em.
[verse 2]
Bean man said there'd be
treasure
So I knew if
I got there in good measure
I'd get no short shrift.

MUSIC: *Polly Wolly Doodle*

CROWN

Couldn't you have bet the
Giant's upset,
You're lookin' an' a-tookin'
all his gold?

JACK

No, I thought he was
a joking cuss,

With mouldy oldy gold,
I been told.
So I say, what the hey,
I'll grab the golden stuff,
For I didn't want a hassle
When I went up to his castle,
Takin' mouldy oldy goldy
each day.

CROWN
[verse 2]
Had you also found
he was joking 'round
When bargin' and a-chargin'
he came
Down the beanstalk fierce
with a staring pierce?

JACK
Yes, surely, but demurely
all the same.
Knew darn well, I could tell
The Friendly Giant does play
I didn't need his c.v. for
I'd seen him on the TV,
Knew that mouldy oldy gold
he gave away.

MUSIC: *I'm a Little Teapot*

CROWN
So you would resort to have
this court
Think the Giant was the
"Friendly" sort?

JACK
Sure I would, of course,
I understand
His crankiness, he got
canned.

CROWN
[verse 2]
But the Friendly Giant
wasn't green.

JACK
That's true, but mould
it could have been;
His castle was damp as the
dickens,
And the gold easy pickings.

MUSIC: *Baa-Baa, Black Sheep*

CROWN
So, young man, you still
believe that you
Were not wrong in your
gold coup?

JACK

Wrong is a really relative
term;
I say, if it feels good,
nobody should squirm.

CROWN

Is that why you went and
dealt a chop
To earthward the Giant drop?

JACK

[verse 2]
Quite right, I was just having
some fun,
Didn't want to hurt no one.

CROWN

Did you not think it
slightly awry?
After all, the poor guy
was 40 storeys high?

JACK

Heck, no, I've read giants
can't get sore.

CROWN

That's it, I will ask no more.

(Crown sits. Clerk #2 indicates that Jack is free do go. Jack whistles on his way back to his seat next to his counsel. Defence rises.)

MUSIC: *Old King Cole*

DEFENCE

So this ends the case
for the defence;
End of the defence case
this be.

Act III

MUSIC: *Old King Cole* (continued)

JUDGE

So the next event
Is closing argument,
And then it's over to the jury.
Start with the Crown's side,
Then the Defence bide,
Last, over to the jury.

MUSIC: *Amazing Grace*

CROWN

Amazing case we've heard
just now:
Jack took coins, harp
and goose;
The Crown says there's
no real big doubt
Of guilt of the accused.

[verse 2]
The Giant never wanted Jack
To take any gold, he said;
He even tried to get them
back
And got chopped down
instead.

MUSIC: *La Cucaracha*

So Jack is guilty, really
quite guilty
There's no doubt he did
the thing.
There's no dissension
'bout his intention,
In a guilty verdict bring!

(The Crown sits down, with just a hint of smugness. In the audience, Giant nods vigorously. From his seat, Jack shakes his head emphatically. Defence counsel rises.)

MUSIC: *All Things Bright and Beautiful*

DEFENCE
Jack is rightly innocent;
He didn't steal, not he;
To rob Giant, he never meant,
So the boy should go free.
He got some beans in
a trade talk;
He thought he was a
business whiz,
So when he climbed up
the beanstalk,
He thought the gold was his.
[verse 2]
Jack did not intend to rob
the Giant;
He's still young and little.
I say that my poor confused
client
Should receive an acquittal.

(Defence counsel sits down and is slapped on the back by an obviously concurring Jack.)

MUSIC: *Overture from Carmen* by Georges Bizet

JUDGE
Is Jack guilty or not guilty
Of the charges of robbery?
Is he guilty or not guilty?
That is what we will ask
of the jury.

CROWN
He is guilty!

DEFENCE
He's not guilty!

CROWN & DEFENCE
Of the charges of robbery.

CROWN
He is guilty!

DEFENCE
He's not guilty!

JUDGE
Listen you all, and we
shall see.

MUSIC: *Twinkle, Twinkle, Little Star*

Jury members, here's a guide
On the point you
must decide.
You have heard the evidence
As to guilt or innocence.
If you've no doubt Jack did it,
Then your verdict must
convict.
[verse 2]
If you doubt his guilt a bit
Then you must young Jack
acquit.
So think about what
you've heard
And if you believe Jack's
word.
Now I'll ask you by
command
To decide by show of hands.

(The jury converse briefly among themselves. As one, they indicate a unanimous thumbs-up for Jack.)

JUDGE
Jury members, your decree
Is that Jack is not guilty.

(Jack jumps up and exultantly high-fives Defence counsel, then darts to the jury box and dispenses gold coins to the jurors.)

MUSIC: *Frère Jacques*

JUDGE
Jack's not guilty.

CLERKS
Jack's not guilty.

JUDGE
So it seems.

CLERKS
So it seems.

JUDGE
He can head back home now…

CLERKS
He can head back home now…

JUDGE
And eat beans.

CLERKS
And eat beans.

(The cast proceeds to sing the lines to the tune of *Frère Jacques* in the round, starting with the Judge and Clerks, then Crown and the Giant, followed by Defence and Jack, then the jury.)

MUSIC: *Symphony No. 5* by Ludwig van Beethoven

CLERKS
Order in court!
Order in court!

(All rise. The judge exits. Jack throws kisses to the audience.)

THE END

Rules for running a modern correctional facility

Source
Reggie Vautour

Occupation
Pension fund administrator

Residence
Ottawa, Ontario

Motto
"One for you, one for me; one for you, two for me; one for you, three for me..."

Rules

1 In keeping with the mandate to make the transition to the facility as smooth as possible, inmates—that is, *guests*—may choose from two styles of uniform: Gucci or Dior.

2 It is important that no guest be treated more leniently than any other. Fillet mignon for everybody!

3 A crisply made bed, cleared dishes and an improved overhand serve substantially qualify guests for the Early Release Program (ERP). But under no circumstances will any guest be eligible for full parole until at least two hours after their initial check-in.

4 No restrictions on visitors, except that a guest's former partners and clients must post a $10,000 bond, pass through an extra metal detector and be supervised at all times, for the safety and comfort of the guest.

5 Guests are expected to assist in the smooth and efficient operation of the facility, by providing detailed specifications of their preferred brands of caviar, the age and origin of their favourite dessert wines, and their choice of truffle filling for their nightly "pillow treat."

6 Remember that justice must not only be done, but appear to be done. Therefore, all guests are asked to limit themselves to no more than four afternoons per week on the facility golf course. There will be absolutely no exceptions—unless they ask really nicely.

Legal foreplay

39

Why the official sport of the law involves puttering around

Golf and lawyers were made for each other. The hardy highland game links up with the legal psyche as a matter of course.

The most straightaway reason for the marriage of barristers and birdies is that both golf and law owe their existence to a set of rules, though scholars are wont to give the nod to golf for complexity. The Canadian writer Eric Nicol has noted that golf has more rules than the Catholic Church.

In any case, success at either activity requires playing the fair way, and understanding the wave of regulations and tricks of the trade. For example, selecting a venue or a judge is a lot like picking a club in a game-winning situation, as choosing unwisely could result in the putting-distance burden of proof in a criminal case being driven clear to the next judicial district.

Then there's tradition. The history of golf is linked inextricably to legal lore, as the first recorded reference to the sport is in an act of James II of Scotland in 1457. The edict banned the sport as "unprofitable" after military-age males habitually bowed out of compulsory archery practice for a less patriotic afternoon with their clubs. The bar was not lifted until 1503, when James IV ingeniously married Princess Margaret of England, ending the fighting between their two countries, and consequently, both the need for archery practice and the statutory prohibition on his golf game.

Golf is a perfect way to relieve traditional lawyers' stresses like billing quotas, hysterical clients and payments on the BMW. Out of the bounds of their desks, lawyers can adopt a stance completely different from their office address. Legend has it that Mary, Queen of Scots relieved her legal and other tensions on the green. Of course, that was before she teed someone off and lost her head over *some* kind of slice.

There are not many recorded fatalities among lawyers on the golf course. But given the present glut in the legal market, this is not necessarily a good thing. There have been plenty of strokes, though—probably a lot more than have been recorded. And we won't even get into playable lies.

Golf also represents the natural flip side of a lawyer's refined, artificially controlled environment. Armed only with clubs, balls and cooler-equipped carts, lawyers can get into the heart of nature, aerating the green with their cleats and discovering the dynamics of flying sand and splashing water, while gaily humming ditties like *Git Along, Little Bogey*. The golf course is the perfect microcosm of the eternal battle between man and nature, and lawyers classify the best courses as "challenging" with a reverence usually reserved for supreme court judges.

Finally, golf and law have some common vernacular. For instance, the term "eagle" describes both an exceptionally low score and a highly skilled (though not necessarily bald) lawyer. Well-prepared golfers would consider it criminal not to keep a set of irons, while lawyers' criminal clients were historically kept in them. Both golf scorecards and old Company Acts shares reflect par values. To a golfer, the phrase "in the leather" describes a situation where a putt is close enough to the hole to be conceded, while some members of the family bar would define that phrase as a fashion statement. Suffice to say that there are scores of other examples of legalese and golf jargon jointly rising to the fore.

Drawing on these commonalties, we can follow through with some new ground rules for our legal system.

It seems only natural that the movement to alternate dispute resolution should lead to a round of golf replacing the customary negotiations or court appearances. Wouldn't it be simpler to instruct lawyers to settle legal battles by challenging opposing counsel to a fast 18 holes? Junior lawyers could pick up valuable training by serving as caddies. Queen's Counsel would be entitled to drive bigger and fancier golf carts than anyone else. The final verdict could be tallied at the 19th hole. And clients would benefit the most, as no course this side of Tokyo charges fees that exceed lawyers' hourly rates.

Naturally, this would involve some hazards and some administrative adjustments, but this does not present a handicap. All non-lawyers in the justice system would simply be retrained as golf pros, landscapers or bartenders, depending on their clothing preferences.

Lawyers are bound to be hooked by this plan. It's sporting. It's environmentally friendly. It would certainly play through the enduring love affair between the lawyers' club and the golf club. And perhaps best of all, it would pull the black-gowned duffers ahead of the white-gowned doctors in terms of being most closely matched with the game.

Rules for sitting in your doctor's waiting room

Source
Satoshi Hiroworshipawa

Occupation
Businessman

Residence
Okazaki, Japan

Motto
"Save money, save face."

Rules

1 Under no circumstances must you complain about the age of the magazines. However, mild letters of protest are permissible in regard to reading material predating the Shoguns.

2 Refrain from inquiries as to whether costs paid by the attending physician to dishonourable elements for unspecified security services will be reflected in your medical bill. Such inquiries are undignified.

3 Never advance your position in line, unless the person preceding you is not native, or is either a convicted criminal or a woman. If that person falls into all three categories, then a delicate combination of polite insults and elementary judo is not entirely inappropriate.

4 When a fellow patient leaves the waiting room, rise as a sign of deference. Then assume their place if your present seating receptacle displeases you.

5 If you feel an urgent need to perform an involuntary bodily function, request a surgically sharp object from the supervising attendant and impale yourself in an unobtrusive manner. The need will soon pass.

6 If you grow inordinately weary of waiting, then consider offering discreet cash gifts to the appropriate administrative personnel. If you are found out, then you must resign from the waiting list in disgust, dishonour and disgrace.

'Twas the eve of fishing season…

41

How a real-life renegade angler almost got away

THIS BAITED FORAY INTO MILDLY LYRICAL DEBAUCHERY is based on an actual civil case out of Minnesota in 1961 called Dellwo vs. Pearson, reported at 107 Northwestern Reports 859. As the Ol' Perfesser used to say, you could look it up.

'Twas the eve of fishing season when all through the lake,
Not a creature was biting, not even a hake;
The rods were hung over the stern with caring
In hopes of catching some salmon, trout or herring.
The Dellwos were perched alert in their boat
With visions of fried fins tickling their throats;
The Mrs. with hair and fish nets, the Mr. chugging brew,
Had prayed to Poseidon for just a nibble or two.

When off the starboard side there arose such a roar
That not even the half-dead bait could ignore;
Then by what should their stunned gaze be o'erwhelmed
But a powerboat with 12-year-old Pearson at the helm.

More swiftly than a popgun sped by the young feller,
Entangling Mrs. D's line in his spinning propeller,
So out of her grasp jerked the reel, which flew
Off the hull, through her glasses and in her left baby blue.

"Foul! Negligence!' screeched Mrs. D in despair,
"Young man, you've breached the due standard of care!
"Get a lawyer! Choose a defence! We'll be in touch!
"The judge will decide whether I doth protest too much!"

And then, in a twinkling, the District Court did note
The issue: whether a minor driving a powerboat
Was to be held to the same standard of care
As an adult doing the same thing, had one been there.

"No!" held the Court, while defendant sweetly smiled,
"The boy's duty is less since he's but a child,
"So the standard of care he must follow at this stage
"Is that which is ordinary for kids of like age."

"Curses!" muttered the Dellwos in defiant retort,
"We'll take the punk clear to the Supreme Court!"
So it came to pass in one year and ten
That Minnesota's highest court tried the issue again:

"While minors are entitled to be judged by experience or age,
"Their public duty increases when they choose to engage
"In activities like driving motor vehicles on water or air
"Whose nature necessitate an adult standard of care."

"It would be unfair to the public," concluded the Court,
"If defendant were not held liable for the tort
"Of negligence, which an adult would no doubt face
"Had he mangled said fishing line in young Pearson's place."

So the Dellwos were heard to gloat, ere the Court did damages wish,
"With a catch like this, who the hell needs fish?"

Law-de-da! Lampooning the laws in our lives

Rules for frequenting a nude beach

Source
Eddie Aqaaluk

Occupation
Fisherman, hunter and guide

Residence
Kugluktuk, Nunavut

Motto
"The early bird gets the worm—unless the bait shop beats him to it."

Rules

1. Be discreet at all times. Don't scare your new neighbours with statements like, "Hi there! Mind if I squat?".
2. Take a loincloth along just in case. You don't want to embarrass the seals.
3. Repel nasty ultraviolet rays by slathering your skin with whale blubber. If you're over 400 pounds, watch for stray harpoons.
4. Mind your extremities. Sometimes the young guys get a little careless about where they leave their traplines.
5. If you can't shake the urge to lie naked on a bearskin, make sure the original owner of the skin is dead first.
6. Always take a thick beach blanket along. That perma-frost is murder on the behind.

Ode to a rule-breaker who stopped 'em cold

43

The strange, but true, origin of a luncheon classic

THERE WAS AN OLDE ENGLISHMAN NAMED MONTAGU,
Live at the gambling table he wanted to;
His habit was so horrible
That he demanded meals portable,
Paraded in while he played, undaunted, through.

Since his food had to be swiftly made and carried,
His servants in the kitchen ne'er tarried
And brought him cold roast
Betwixt slices of toast,
So he could sup and ante up unharried.

Combining bread and cold beef proved so hot
That even common folk gave it a shot,
With turkey, vegetables hearty,
Halibut and Havarti,
Toting tons o' filled buns to the tablecloth.

Though the idea did earlier occur,
Montagu's thumb's-up made it *de rigueur*
And while 'twas an unplanned glitch
For the Fourth Earl of Sandwich,
His handle will be served with verve forev*eur.*

Rules for adopting a global currency

Source
Mustafa Hakim

Occupation
Student (State police informant)

Residence
Al Basrah, Iraq

Motto
"Keep the guns, bury the roses."

Rules

1 Invite the delegates to Baghdad. If they need more space for their meeting, we can expand our facilities to Kuwait.

2 Refuse to submit to the Yankee warmongers, who would put Mickey Mouse on the new money, instead of the choice of the people, Saddam Hussein.

3 Ensure everyone agrees on the exchange rates. Those who do not should be executed.

4 As a special consideration to our neighbours in Iran, exchange their coinage for its total weight in camel turds.

5 Have the Swiss safeguard all the money before conversion. Their banking record after the last world war proves they can be trusted.

6 Respect the privacy of nations. If inspectors from the United Nations seek to ensure we have destroyed all banned currencies, tell them to go kiss a viper.

Nine customer service programs being developed by the banks

45

New standards in putting people first

1

COMPLIMENTARY COPIES of the popular lifestyle manual, *The Joy of Overdraft*

2

"Environmental" service charge for breathing recirculated oxygen in branches

3

Catchy ad jingle for home renovation loans: "When new room's in your eye and int'rest rates ain't high, that's a mortgage"

4

Special service for claustrophobic customers: therapy sessions in the vault

5

A contest: "Guess our profits for the year, rounded to the nearest $200 million—win a handsome, chrome-plated pen"

6

New way to reduce waiting time: whenever the customer line-up exceeds 10 people, state-of-the-art heat sensors trigger the fire alarms

7

In-branch dental equipment to melt down gold teeth for collateral

8

A $12-million study to determine how banks can improve their image

9

Glossy calendars featuring "Hot Hunks and Bouncy Babes We've Foreclosed On"

Rules for handling automated bank transactions

Source
Larry and Madge Bogulski

Occupation
Farmers—and proud hockey parents!

Residence
Ruthilda, Saskatchewan

Motto
"Go, Ryley, go!"

Rules

1 If you're at the end of a long line, liven things up by starting a wave.

2 Beat those cravings for nuts 'n' beer. Pack your own in advance, and maybe a couple dozen extra. You might sell enough to pay for next year's team uniform.

3 When you finally get to the machine, resist the urge to check leftover account slips. Take 'em home and look at 'em later!

4 If the machine rejects your card straight off, yell and boo like crazy. Tell the machine, "If you had one more eye, you'd be a Cyclops!" Then demand a second opinion from the nearest goal judge.

5 After three transactions, throw your hat on the floor and cheer like a banshee. If you're anywhere near Detroit, throw an octopus instead.

6 Tell anyone within earshot that your home branch could kick this branch's ass.

High-tech gets hip

47

When science goes to the Oscars

In a culture obsessed with The Next Big Thing, it's astonishing to find the world of science—the rules of which govern us all—ranked somewhere between phlegm futures and nose hair clippings. Since the public pillorying of the harmless pocket protector, research and development (or R & D, its clever and catchy acronym) has become undeniably uncool.

Dr. Bryn Blattz of the University of Dusseldorf at Mannheim, a specialist in such matters and a member of UNESCO's Task Force on Bunsen Burners and Other Neat Stuff, says the lack of fresh bodies is the greatest threat to the scientific community since the advent of the common lab explosion. While Dr. Blattz does work in cryogenics, his remarks underlie the cold, hard reality: R & D needs better PR—and PDQ, if not ASAP.

With the fabled assistance of Degas & Depew, a prominent media and public relations firm out of Two Hole, Wyoming, we can shift the spotlight back to science, where it belongs. If millions can devote what seems like a month to tune in and watch Hollywood hand out cheesy statuettes over mostly mediocre movies, then they should go positively gaga over great performances in real life.

We take you now to our gal about test tube town, May Newton. May?

• • •

It's hard to describe the gravity of this event. The eyes of the global scientific community were on Ernie Coombs Hall here in Tickletrunk, Newfoundland tonight for the 14th Annual High-There-Tech Awards. The hall sure looked funny with all of those eyes on it.

This year's theme, *A Night in Bosnia,* featured the obligatory shelling and looting, but was refreshingly free of the hostage-taking incidents which marred the *Baghdad Follies* episode of 1988.

Backed by a chorus of dancers sporting tasteful teal lab coats, Host Edgar P. Sassafrass BSC, PHD, POSTDOC DIPTHONG launched the evening with a medley of melodies from the high-tech hit parade, including the smoking *My Love's Down the Tubes,* the raga-wracked *Grant Me a Patent, Baby* and the exultant, unrepentent *Paid My Dues with these R & D Blues.*

Leading the fertile crop of award winners was Professor Hortense Q. Zookie-Chong PHD, OK of the Jakarta Institute of Internal Organs, whose brilliant experiments in virtual cardiac technology captured the coveted Best Scientist Award, not to mention the hearts of the judges.

Entrepreneur Roscoe J. "Mookie" Kaalkoo, BA of Fresno, California won the Coolest Discovery Award for his spiralling improvements to the common doorstop. In fact, he was seen recoiling at the podium.

In a surprise development, Jimmy "The Enforcer" Magyarano GRADE 4-1/2, currently in the employ of certain Russian interests, captured the prestigious Boboskowich Prize for his body of work in cement. He also took home the Best Supporting Actor in a Research Lab Award. (He didn't actually *win,* but he grabbed the trophy onstage and nobody felt strongly enough about it to stop him.)

Bright Idea Award winner Candace Cadswalloppe RN of Sacred Liver Hospital in Bordeaux, France charmed the crowd with her humble acceptance speech: "After considerable research, testing and clinical trials, I have concluded—and my findings do tend to support this—that you like me!"

Wall Street doorman Marvin D. Blando BA, BO raised the roof and several eyebrows by sending a robot onstage to claim his prize for Best Choreography of a Science-Related Media Announcement. The robot was notable for its 16 sets of eyebrows—complete with glasses and noses—a curiosity dismissed by farsighted observers as the price of genius.

The cacophonous crowd was on its feet throughout the evening, thanks in no small part to the organizers' brazen theme, *New Horizons in Whoopie-Cushions.* However, some disgruntled attendees claimed they would not stand for it next year.

Organizers are already hard at work on the 15th Annual, which is rumoured to feature a Sumo squatting theme, together with a celebration of the state of flatness.

Now, a word from your local bottler of Klingon Kola, the beverage that *will* stick to most dental work.

Rules for livening up meetings of your local Lions Club

Source

H9437

Occupation

Gunner, Zotlan Empire

Residence

Space, 24th century

Motto

"Your suicide pill or mine?"

Rules

1 Spit up salsa over crudely drawn caricatures of "sissy" Lions from lesser galaxies.

2 Frequent washrooms under the guise of an invisibility beam and make rude noises.

3 Substitute plutonium crystals for sugar at the coffee table.

4 Exchange highly dangerous, exploding business cards.

5 After electing members to next year's executive, teleport them to sub-arctic penal colonies.

6 Impale the guy in the Spock suit at skit night.

Research mysteries, episodes I & II

49

A baffling case of duplicity, purloined trade secrets and extra paperwork

Episode I

THIS IS THE RESEARCH LAB. My name is Shelby Krankenheimer-Psmythe. I'm a scientist. Friday morning, 8:15 a.m.: call comes in from the director of R & D. I charge up my electric cart and pop wheelies all the way to her office. Being a prototype, the thing runs out of juice after only five feet, so I get out and walk the last three.

"Another strange one for you, Professor."

"Give me all of the details, Chief," I say. Being a devout empiricist, I just want to get the facts.

"As you know, the organization is about to launch our latest product. It's a secret. A big secret. So big a secret, in fact, that even the product designers don't know what it is."

I pull out a pack of bubble gum cigars and offer her one, but she's too chewed up to notice.

"This morning, we got some dirt from one of our agents, working undercover as a janitor at our toughest competitor, Fabs Labs & Deli. He says they're about to scoop our new product."

"Gee, Chief, that's against the rules," I mutter in a measured voice.

"Right," she coughs compliantly. "I want you to infiltrate their shop, find out what's going on, bring back any stolen trade secrets, destroy any infringing materials, and then write up the whole episode in a scholarly article. Our publication credits are down by 18 per cent this quarter."

"Got it, Chief. You want fresh ground pepper with that?"

Her black look and return to her Rubik's Cube tell me it was time to take a powder.

Back in my office, I ring up my pal, "Eagle Eyes" Sumatra. Although EE flies by the seat of his pants, he's always at my beak and call. We agree to flock to Fabs.

Cleverly disguised as visiting academics from Digby, Nova Scotia (the lobster pennants fool them every time), EE and I quickly gain access to Fabs' plant and head directly for the nerve centre of any decent research organization: the cafeteria. It's coffee time, and the place is packed tighter than a clinical testing budget.

After picking up a couple of really ugly green kiwi 'n' lime punches, we each join a table and act real nonchalant. That's when our good luck runs out.

No sooner do I park my posterior than I feel a tap on my shoulder. Actually, it's more like a knockout punch. To be more precise, it misses my shoulder and finds the back of my head. I hit the lino like a ton of grant application forms. Although my bifocals are thrown clear, I can distinctly make out a huge, grossly overweight figure in a lab coat, hovering over me like a Hiroshima cloud.

"You're coming with us," it explodes. When I gently try to demur, an army of hands grabs my arms and drags me out.

Is this really the end for Professor Shelby Krankenheimer-Psmythe? What unknown evil awaits our hero in the bowels of Fabs Labs & Deli? Will Eagle Eyes swoop to his rescue? Will they get what they came for in time? And will they leverage the experience into a PR coup and further R & D tax credits? Stay tuned for the startling answers!

Intermission:
Five fine gifts for the scientist who has everything

Spandex lab coat to promote more exercise on the job

Coupon booklet entitling bearer to 10 free patent applications

Study grant to research ergonomics of lying on warm, sandy beaches for extended periods during the winter

Popular gag gift: open-ended test tubes

The real truth behind Who pudding

And now, back to Research mysteries…

Episode II

This is a broom closet. My name is Shelby Krankenheimer-Psmythe. I'm a scientist. Friday afternoon, 12:58 p.m.:I'm sitting with my knees up my nose, bound and gagged somewhere in the bowels of Fabs Labs & Deli, where our arch-rivals have locked me up. They're trying to stop me from stopping them from scooping our new top-secret product, in flagrant violation of the law and in fragrant violation of common scents.

I don't know what's worse: failing in my mission, or being apprehended in the cafeteria before I could go back for the Double-glazed, Upside-down Kiwi Truffle Supreme™. As I contemplate slicing through the ropes with my rapier-like wit, the door is thrown open, and another fine embodiment of Darwin's theories yanks me out by the collar, slaps my bifocals back on and hands me a stack of "Captured Enemy Agent" forms to complete in triplicate.

"It's curtains for you now, egg brain," he guffaws, slapping me into a fetid shower stall, untying my hands and tossing me a badly chewed HB pencil. When I ask him if he doesn't mean egg-*head*, he cracks up and poaches a line from Dr. Sim.

I complete the forms and ace the quiz on the periodic table on page 17.

"Awright, Krankencase. Now you see the boss."

Hot dog! A confrontation with the evil fiend masterminding the heist of our new product was something I'd been relishing.

Unwittingly completing my doomed disguise as a visiting academic from Digby with a blindfold reeking of rancid herring, the burly behemoth spins me around three times and hands me something with a point at the end. At first I think it's another pencil, but it turns out to be a donkey's tail. Apparently, my host has some unresolved issues around old birthday party games.

After a few pointed efforts at getting to the bottom of the matter, I am ushered in to a cavernous corner office. My jaw sags at the dazzling array of research awards, plaques and cheesy Einstein posters adorning the walls. My jaw drops to the subbasement when the swivel-chair rotates to reveal the research director of Fabs—none other than my most trusted pal, "Eagle Eyes" Sumatra.

"You rat!" I howl. "You weasel! You Phoenician in Pharaoh's clothing!"

"Tut, tut," he coos, as I go mum. "Never underestimate the extraordinary R & D opportunities afforded by double agency."

As he launches into a protracted discourse on the funding conditions which led him to the table at Fabs Labs & Deli, I counter with a smirk.

"Do not mock me, you chicken," he clucks, coldly cutting the air with a slide-rule. "Either you give us all of your trade secrets, or..."

I implore him not to say it. But of course, he does anyway.

"Or I use my contacts to ship you back to that grade eight science lab, until you get permanent Bazooka Joe stains on your lab coat!"

At this, my cheeks blanch, my knees buckle and I collapse face-first into a dish of tongue depressers on his desk.

Will Professor Shelby Krankenheimer-Psmythe sell out? And if he does, will he be able to leverage the experience into a published paper and a research grant? Stay tuned to future books for the startling answers!

Rules for looking good and feeling fit

Source
Juniper Cho

Occupation
Computer programmer

Residence
Vancouver, British Columbia

Motto
"Get more RAM, man."

Rules

1 Scan in a recent photo of yourself and knock off pounds electronically.

2 Tired of unsightly butt overhang? Get a bigger chair!

3 Don't be a lab rat all day. Get some fresh air once in awhile—but don't forget to take the laptop.

4 The Hacker's Diet: sugar-free cola by the gigabyte.

5 Find yourself a screen-saver with a picture of the sun on it, and get a virtual tan. No harmful UV rays!

6 The no-fail solution: upgrade your RAM—before you forget why you need to be fit in the first place.

Trash of the titans

51

The screenplay
where litter is not
just another
throwaway

FADE IN:

EXTERIOR ("EXT.") CITY HALL – DAY

A small but determined group of ENVIRONMENTAL ACTIVISTS, sporting long grey hair and granola-flavoured attire, marches in protest outside City Hall. Their placards say things like *Plant trees, not trash, Bring back clean air* and *Don't be a chump, can the new dump.* Among the group are mid-fiftyish BRETT BACKUS and BLANCHE BACKUS, who wear distinctive necklaces with amulets depicting a tree.

ACTIVISTS
Down with the dump! Down with the dump!

Overlooking the scene, TYLER PRITZLAFF lurks behind a huge billboard. He wears a small black earring, and scratches his armpit to reveal a tattoo on his arm depicting a tree inside a circle with a diagonal red slash across it. He unscrews some fasteners, causing the billboard to topple earthward.

ACTIVISTS (CONT'D)
Help! Look out!

The billboard lies on the ground. Several pairs of inert, sandal-sporting legs stick out from under it. The stunned survivors hold their protest signs more limply than before. Tyler laughs, tosses gum wrappers and pop cans off the side of the building, makes his escape.

EXT. FUNERAL PARLOUR – DAY

A devastated, serious-looking, very clean-cut BART BACKUS (30), son of Brett and Blanche, emerges from a building marked *Figby's Fast Funerals.* He pauses at the railing outside the entrance, sniffs, removes his late parents' amulets from his coat pocket and stares at them intently.

DISSOLVE TO:

EXT. FOREST – DAY (20 YEARS EARLIER)

A rustic log cabin in a heavily wooded area, with a sign bearing the words *Yohoho National Park* tacked onto a tree. YOUNG BART BACKUS takes the daily trash to a lovingly cultivated compost heap. His parents, a younger Brett and Blanche, gaze approvingly at his efforts from the cabin window.

DISSOLVE TO:

EXT. FUNERAL PARLOUR – DAY

Bart wipes away a silent tear, returns the amulets to his pocket, looks down at the pavement. As the wind sweeps a swirling circle of crumpled candy bar wrappers and fetid french fry envelopes around his feet, he clenches his fist and gazes heavenward.

BART
That ties it. From now on, I dedicate my life to fighting grime.

Several other MOURNERS emerge from the building, including JASON JACKSON, a teenaged orphan of the billboard catastrophe.

BART (CONT'D)
How are you doing, sport?

Jason shrugs.

BART (CONT'D)
Name's Backus. Bart Backus.

JASON
Jason Jackson.

BART
Feel like a bean curd shake?

JASON
Why not, Scott.

Bart registers pleasant surprise at finding a fellow health fan in his time of grief.

INTERIOR ("INT.") FERN GROTTO CAFE – DAY

Bart and Jason sit at a fern-festooned eatery, tucking into bean curd shakes, organic french fries and a communal plate of alfalfa sprouts.

BART
So what do you want out of life, kid?

JASON

That's an easy one, Mon. I want to make the world a cleaner place. I want to rid the earth of waste and smog, Bog. And after I do all of that, I want to meet great women. (beat) How about you?

BART

Jason, I have this dream. I'm no longer a quiet environmentalist, content to dream big and live small. (beat) I am the avenger of all things rotten. The vigilante of vileness. The wazoo of waste.

Jason stops in mid-french fry and stares incredulously.

BART (CONT'D)

Jason, our cities are a blight of discarded debris, cast-off clutter and rotting refuse. (beat) I see it as my sacred trust to make the city clean and pretty again. And to make sure every citizen plays by the rules.

JASON

Okay, Jose.

BART

Mom and Dad would have wanted it that way. And Jason, I have a plan.

JASON

What's the deal, Neil?

Bart maps out his plan on the tabletop, using utensils and organic seasoning shakers to illustrate. Eventually, Jason joins in. They nod in agreement from time to time.

JASON

So there's our battle plan, Stan.

BART

Jason?

JASON

Yeah?

BART

Do you always end every other sentence with a rhyme?

JASON

You got it, Britt. It helps me focus.

Bart shakes his head, eyes Jason.

BART

So are we partners?

JASON

We sure are, Jafar.

They give each other a high-five, and seal their partnership by smearing ketchup on their own wrists, touching each other's wrists together, then carefully cleaning the mottled ketchup off their own wrists with french fries.

SERIES OF SHOTS:

A) Bart and Jason sit in the public library, surrounded by monolithic piles of books, intently boning up on titles like *Waste Management Made E-Z, Garbage For Beginners* and *Business Recycle Theory.*

B) At the city dump, Bart and Jason, garbed in garish green sweats, run up huge mountains of refuse, run through two long rows of tattered tires laid side by side, leap over junked appliances.

C) At the city offices, a smiling Bart, dressed in an ill-fitting suit, shakes the hand of the PERSONNEL DIRECTOR at the Department of Sanitation, Parks and Recreation, and receives a coveted Sanitation staff radio. The director removes a *Help Wanted* notice from the wall.

D) Bart and Jason, garbed in garish seamstress's attire, sew a pair of khaki costumes, complete with capes and tree-shaped logo reminiscent of Brett and Blanche's amulets. In the background are two large sketches of the outfits, bearing the legends, *The Bagman* and *Twist-Tie Kid.*

INT. BART'S KITCHEN – NIGHT

Bart and Jason congregate around a solitary candle on a teetering table. Bart's parents' amulets surround the candle.

BART & JASON

We vow to bring garbage to justice. And to always segregate the recyclable stuff.

INT. BART'S KITCHEN – NIGHT (LATER)

Bart and Jason sit at the kitchen table, playing Parcheesi, listening to Bart's Sanitation department radio. The voice of Sanitation Commissioner MACDRECK crackles over the airwaves.

MACDRECK
(OFFSCREEN, "O.S.")
Attention all units. Large stink bomb exploded at Munsinger Elementary. Forensics is on the scent, but they need help.

Bart and Jason jump up, race to adjoining closets to change. They lock themselves in.

INT. BART'S KITCHEN – NIGHT (LATER)

Bart and Jason sit at the kitchen table, playing tiddlywinks, listening to Bart's radio.

MACDRECK (O.S.)
Attention all units. Major paper blizzard blowing out of Reese's Recycling. Staff are shuffling over there now, but they need more help.

Again, Bart and Jason jump up, race to adjoining closets to change. They emerge sheepishly, wearing each other's ill-fitting costumes.

INT. BART'S KITCHEN – NIGHT (LATER)

Bart and Jason sit at the kitchen table, playing tick-tack-toe, listening to Bart's radio.

MACDRECK (O.S.)
Attention all units. Serious mess over by the elephants' compound at the zoo. Cleanup team's trickling over there now, but they need more backup.

Once again, Bart and Jason jump up, race to adjoining closets to change. They emerge (this time in correct costumes) and bolt out the door. They return to tidy up hastily, then run out again. They come back once more to turn out the lights before leaving for good.

INT. LAVANGS' KITCHEN – DAY

In a disgusting den of languishing leftovers and dusty disarray, Bart's dishevelled next door neighbour, LUCIUS LAVANG, squints and stares between venetian blinds at the window. Lucius' equally slothful wife, LAVERNE LAVANG, sits at a table, filing her nails and chain-smoking a huge cigar.

LUCIUS
Can you believe that guy?

LAVERNE
What's he doing now, my big day-old dumpling? Vacuuming his lawn again? Blowing dust off his roof with a straw? Polishing his rock garden?

She cackles crazily.

LUCIUS
Can't make it out too good, my fermented little sugar plum. But he seems to be running out to his garage in his long underwear... (beat) and some kind of blanket fluttering in the breeze behind him.

Laverne absently places her lit cigar on the tablecloth. She moves to the window beside Lucius and peers out.

LAVERNE
He's got some weirdo punk with him.

LUCIUS
You know, I've about had it with his clean and tidy behaviour.

Lucius spits on the floor.

LUCIUS (CONT'D)
If he ain't trespassing on other people's lawns to pick weeds, he's composting enough sludge to fertilize from here to Alpha Centauri. (beat) We've got to fix this guy.

LAVERNE
He's giving the neighbourhood a bad name.

Laverne sniffs the air loudly, oblivious to the plume of smoke rising from the burning tablecloth behind her.

LAVERNE (CONT'D)
Do you smell something burning in here?

SERIES OF SHOTS:

A) The Bagman and Twist-Tie Kid patrol the moonlit streets in the Bagmobile, a cacophony of buckets, mops, brooms, cleaning fluids and above all, bags.

B) At a busy crossing, Bagman and Twist-Tie Kid scoop up and bag a deposit made by a doddering basset hound. They're thanked by a kindly OLD LADY.

C) *The Burghers' Bugle* rolls off the press, bearing the headline, "Masked Twosome Bag Trash on Legislature Lawn, Save Royal Visit Embarrassment."

D) In a brief but touching ceremony, the MAYOR of Burgherville gives our heroes the keys to the city dump.

E) The next edition of the *Bugle* rolls off the press, bearing the headline, "City Becoming Pretty Again."

EXT. NEWSSTAND – DAY

A menacing figure stands on a street corner, reading the *Bugle*. He lowers the paper, revealing an anti-tree tattoo on his arm. Tyler strokes his chin and snarls.

INT. FERN GROTTO CAFE – NIGHT

Bart and Jason chew over a plate of some swamp-like substance. Bart produces two heat sensors, with corresponding homing devices.

JASON
What've you got there, Pierre?

BART
Heat-sensors, kid. Hook onto the waistband of our underwear. If one of us is in tough, the sensor will activate the other's homing device.

Bart's Sanitation department radio beeps like a roadrunner on steroids.

MACDRECK (O.S.)
Attention all units. Disastrous garbage spill on Brzynowitz Bridge. Fresh hatch of flies there, too. Our SWAT team is heading over, but they'll come up flat without help.

Bart and Jason dash from the scene.

EXT. BRIDGE – NIGHT

The Bagmobile sputters up to the scene of the spill in the pouring rain. A city garbage truck lies toppled. Garbage flows everywhere. Traffic is clogged at both ends of the bridge. Car horns honk. Bagman and Twist-Tie Kid get the once-over from incredulous MOTORISTS and the CITY CREW.

BAGMAN
The cycle. And get the pump.

TWIST-TIE KID
Will do, Stu.

The duo race to the rear of the Bagmobile, emerge on Bart's late parents' two-seater bicycle and pedal along the narrow sidewalk along the bridge. When they reach a position parallel to the toppled garbage truck, they vault the railing dividing the sidewalk from the bridge road and sprint towards the spill. Twist-Tie Kid lugs a large pump and twist-ties. Bagman's belt dangles bags like commando kite tails.

They glance at each other, nod in unison and go to work: they pump garbage into bags, secure the bags and ferry them by cycle to the city trucks waiting at either end of the bridge.

EXT. BRIDGE – NIGHT (LATER)

The cleanup complete, our heroes examine the overturned Sanitation vehicle.

BAGMAN
Take a look at this, kid.

The Bagman indicates the perpetrators' trademark, a peculiar anti-tree logo tattooed onto the windshield.

TWIST-TIE KID
A deliberate act of sabotage, Raj.

BAGMAN
Right as rain. I overheard one of the crew say he spotted some punks leaving the scene in a big hurry.

They look at each other pensively.

INT. MACDRECK'S OFFICE – DAY

Bagman and the Twist-Tie Kid barrel into the office, where MacDreck reads *The Burghers' Bugle.* The headline blares, "Boundless Bagman, Boy Buddy, Baffle Burg Brigade by Blitzing Bridge Bilge Barrage."

BAGMAN
What's up, Commissioner?

MACDRECK
The results of our investigation are in. I don't like it one bit.

Our heroes stare at each other grimly.

MACDRECK (CONT'D)
We believe that both the spill on the bridge and the rash of littering are the work of the force behind the anti-tree logo. (beat) The filthiest fiends the city has ever known.

TWIST-TIE KID
Well, soak my squeegie, Luigi. We suspected as much.

BAGMAN
We've seen their work. But we've never battled them face to face.

MACDRECK
Sure, we can handle general rubbish and the odd toxic spill. But taking on an underground network of nihilistic misfits is like walking into a porcupine den buck naked.

MacDreck perches on his desk.

MACDRECK (CONT'D)
In the naked city, the porcupines call themselves the Metropolitan Association of Listless, Littering, Bored, Rage-filled and Tree-hating Survivors. The MALL-BRATS.

They regard each other silently at this ominous news.

INT. SCHOOL BATHROOM – DAY

The mother of all MALLBRATS—their leader, none other than Tyler—dumps heavily on a dozen MEMBERS of his motley Mafia.

TYLER

You incompetent dolts! A freakin' kindergarten job! We'll never jump from strip malls to municipal infrastructure with results like that.

MALLBRAT #1

But boss, we'd-a done a lot more damage if those costumed goody two-shoes hadn't shown up.

TYLER

That does it. Everywhere I go, everything I hear, is The Bagman and his spic-and-span sidekick.

Tyler pulls an earring off MALLBRAT #2, who doubles over, clutching his ear.

MALLBRAT #2

Yeeeooooooow!

The other MALLBRATS shift uneasily. Tyler dismisses them with a wave. They shuffle out, obviously relieved. Tyler stares into a mirror, deep in thought. He strokes his jaw and absent-mindedly touches his black earring. Stirred by this, he stares at his reflection.

DISSOLVE TO:

SERIES OF SHOTS (YEARS EARLIER)

A) YOUNG TYLER is put down to play near a pile of dirt by his mother, PRISCILLA, who wears prominent earrings.

B) Young Tyler, unwashed and in filthy clothes, walks into a schoolyard carrying a battered lunch pail, and is shunned and jeered by various CHILDREN.

C) At a dance in a gym festooned with a banner reading *Good luck, graduates of Gerda Munsinger Elementary School,* a grossly filthy Young Tyler spills slime over his dancing CLASSMATES, delighting in their horrified reaction.

DISSOLVE TO:

INT. SCHOOL BATHROOM – DAY (PRESENT)

Shrugging off his flashback, Tyler tugs at his ear and snarls at his reflection.

TYLER

I don't like to see the results of a night's work tidied up all nice in durable, industrial-strength bags. And I don't like to read 48-point headlines about psycho clean-freaks. (beat) But I do like getting revenge.

EXT. NEWSSTAND – DAY

Two figures stand at the same street corner as Tyler did earlier, reading the *Bugle.* On the back page of each newspaper is an ad bearing the headline, "Wanted: MALLBRATS seek info on The Bagman. Big bucks reward."

In unison, they turn over their newspapers to face the back page ad, then lower the papers. They are Bart and Jason.

BART
Quite the ad. Must have cost a pile.

JASON
But who'd be low enough to do business with a MALLBRAT, Matt?

INT. LAVANGS' KITCHEN – DAY

Lucius and Laverne sit at the table opposite Tyler. MALLBRATS #1 and #2 stand subserviently behind Tyler.

LUCIUS
(to Laverne)
My fetid little mushroom, this is Tyler Pritzlaff. And these must be MALLBRATS.

LAVERNE
Charmed, I'm sure.

TYLER
Let's cut to the chase. You said you could deliver The Bagman.

LAVERNE
We have a very strong suspicion about who he is. (to Lucius) Don't we, my precious, rotten apricot?

LUCIUS
Yeah. Like she said. Yeah.

TYLER
So what are your terms?

LUCIUS
You guys give us four grand down, and another ten when we give you The Bagman.

LAVERNE
And don't forget the sales tax. We run a reputable consulting group here.

TYLER
Two grand down. Another eight later. And no GST. I don't want to go over my withholding quota this quarter.

LUCIUS
Three grand down. Another twelve later. And two-thirds of the tax.

TYLER
Hey! That's more than you wanted the first time!

LAVERNE
Sorry, sonny. We're consultants, not accountants.

TYLER
Three grand down, another nine later. You eat the tax, but you get 25 class "B" common, non-voting shares in our Seattle subsidiary, MALLBRATS (Pacific Northwestern) Limited. Our lawyers hold it in trust. Are you in?

LUCIUS
(to Laverne)
My infested little papaya?

LAVERNE
Yeah, we're in.

EXT. LAVANGS' HOUSE – DAY

Tyler and his cohorts toss litter on the Lavangs' lawn as they leave.

MALLBRAT #1
They'd take this garbage as a compliment.

MALLBRAT #2
(in high-pitched voice, after his ear-pull)
They should. There's a refund on the empties.

TYLER
Boys, go tail our new business associates. If they lead you to The Bagman, we'll bag him ourselves.

MALLBRATS #1 & #2
Okay, boss.

EXT. BART'S BACKYARD – NIGHT

Laverne, toting a large butterfly net and a very large can clearly labelled *ACME Knockout Gas,* darts from bush to bush from her house to Bart's back porch.

INT. BART'S KITCHEN – NIGHT

Bart and Jason graze on a grotesque vegetarian creation while Laverne peers in through the back door window, with a view to entering. Repulsed, she drops back out of view. Oblivious, our heroes keep eating.

INT. CITY OFFICES – DAY

At work, Bart senses that he's being watched, but does not see Lucius and Laverne furtively following him with large butterfly nets.

EXT. CITY PARK – DAY

Bart eats his lunch in a serene, pristine park. Just as he rises to leave, the butterfly net-wielding Lucius and Laverne lunge at him from opposite sides. A moment too late, they net each other, unseen by a still oblivious Bart.

EXT. BART'S BACKYARD – NIGHT

Lucius, toting a large butterfly net and a gun labelled *ACME Instant Tranquilizer,* waddles between bushes from his house to Bart's back porch.

INT. BART'S KITCHEN – NIGHT

Bart and Jason graze on an even more grotesque vegetarian creation than the night before, while Lucius peers through the back door window. Repulsed but forewarned, he removes a packet labelled *ACME Stomach Stabilizer,* pops two pills and enters the kitchen.

LUCIUS
Good evening, men.

Bart gazes at Lucius' dishevelled appearance with great pity.

BART
Mr. Lavang. Can I do some laundry for you again, sir?

LUCIUS
That does it.

Lucius unearths the gun from his armpit, points it at Bart and pulls the trigger, only to have a stick pop out, from which a flag unrolls, bearing the word *Bang.*

LUCIUS (CONT'D)
No wonder they let me have it without registration.

Bart and Jason stare at him, astonished. A half-digested, seaweed-like substance slithers out of Jason's gaping mouth. Lucius storms out the back door, muttering under his breath. Jason re-inserts the errant food.

JASON
What a strange person, Thurston. Are all your neighbours like this?

EXT. BART'S GARAGE – NIGHT

Believing they are unobserved, Bagman and Twist-Tie Kid push the Bagmobile silently out of the garage. Unknowingly, they run over the feet of Lucius and Laverne (who are hiding in the bushes), and plow through a large, makeshift butterfly net rigged between two trees. Watching the scene from behind some decrepit lawn ornaments on the Lavangs' lawn are MALLBRATS #1 and #2, who take notes.

EXT. TWIST-TIE STORE – NIGHT

The Bagmobile parks outside a large store bearing a sign, *Ollie's Twist-tie Palace* and a smaller sign, *Buy 2 tons, get 1 free.* Bagman waits outside when his radio goes off.

MACDRECK (O.S.)
Attention, all units. Monstrous grease spill at Burgherville Burgers on Bun Boulevard. Our kitchen crew has it on the front-burner, but they're fried. Get over there.

Bagman glances into the store, at the radio, back to the store.

BAGMAN
I hate it when he stops to try the samples. (beat) I've got to go.

He jumps into the Bagmobile and zooms off.

EXT. BURGER STAND – NIGHT

As Bagman parks, MALLBRATS emerge from other vehicles to litter at a feverish pitch, handily overcoming Bagman's attempts to pick up after them. After a brief but fervent struggle, the crew overpowers Bagman, ties him up and delivers him to a defiant Tyler.

TYLER
So we meet at last, Mister Bagman.

BAGMAN
I should have known.

TYLER
Known what, white teeth?

BAGMAN
I'd take a lot of crap from you.

TYLER
I do the jokes here, begonia breath.

At a signal from Tyler, MALLBRAT #1 dumps a bucket full of oozing, rancid slime over Bagman's head.

TYLER (CONT'D)
(sniffs)
Gee, something stinks. And you know what, Bags? I think it's you!

Tyler and the MALLBRATS laugh raucously.

BAGMAN
If you're going to do the jokes, you're going to have to do better than that.

TYLER
Yeah? Then try this one on for size, you big psycho.

On command, MALLBRAT #2 dumps a bag of TRASH over Bagman's head. Much of it sticks to his new coat of ooze.

BAGMAN
Was it something I said?

TYLER
Let me tell you something, Mr. Close-cropped nose hair. Your crusade for niceness and prettiness makes me ill. It makes us all ill.

The MALLBRATS murmur their assent.

TYLER (CONT'D)
It's because idiots like you keep up the myth of a squeaky-keen world that guys like me have to stand up and say enough!

The Bagman nods sympathetically at Tyler's rage.

TYLER (CONT'D)
This isn't the Fifties anymore, you know. All that nuclear family stuff was garbage. And I mean, real garbage.

At a signal from Tyler, various MALLBRATS pelt Bagman with soiled disposable diapers.

TYLER (CONT'D)
So we're giving it all back to you. Literally. Me and the MALLBRATS. We're going to keep dumping on this lovely, homogenized, white bread world of yours.

Tyler is in the face of Bagman, who winces from the stench.

TYLER (CONT'D)
And that's why I get a special thrill out of flattening those green dork-head protesters. Great gimmick, huh?

Bagman is jolted, realizing that it was Tyler who did in Brett, Blanche and Jason's parents at the protest march.

BAGMAN
(under his breath)
Mom! Dad!

TYLER
But enough about me. Let's talk about you. In the past tense, that is. You've gotten in my way for the last time.

(to MALLBRATS)
Toss him in the dumpster and bury him 'til he suffocates.

At Tyler's signal, the ruffians drag Bagman away.

BAGMAN
(under his breath)
What a dirty way to die, Hy. (beat) Nuts. The kid's got *me* doing it now.

MALLBRAT #2
Boss, you sure this is cool? We waste him, and every Sanitation dick in town will be on our case.

TYLER
Hmm. (beat) Hold it, boys! I've got an even more wicked idea!

Tyler produces a cellular phone, hits a speed-dial button and whispers into it enthusiastically.

EXT. TWIST-TIE STORE – NIGHT

Emerging from the store with three cavernous crateloads of twist-ties, Twist-Tie Kid hears a ringing signal from his pocket. He pulls out the heat sensor and waves frantically at passing vehicles.

TWIST-TIE KID
Taxi! Taxi! (under his breath)
Always wanted to do that.

In short order, a cab, driven by DRIVER, screeches to a halt beside him, just missing his feet.

TWIST-TIE KID (CONT'D)
Know the way to Burgherville Burgers?

DRIVER
Mack, around here, they call me Hound of the Burghervilles.

The cab screeches off, barely giving Kid time to get in.

EXT. BURGER STAND – NIGHT

As Tyler shuts his cellphone, a white van rolls up. Three burly ORDERLIES grapple with Bagman, strap him to a stretcher, inject a sedative and load him onto the van.

TYLER
You're gonna love this, Bags. I knew you were nuts when I first saw you, on that anti-litter video. Now the world will know, too.

The back doors of the van close to reveal the words *Sigmund's Semi-private Sanitarium.* The MALLBRATS laugh uproariously as the van pulls out of the park.

EXT. BURGER STAND – NIGHT

Twist-Tie Kid arrives to find the drive-in deserted. He surveys the litter and the tell-tale signs of the struggle, and looks completely hopeless.

EXT. CITY PARK – NIGHT

Against the backdrop of a clock tower indicating 3:00 a.m., Tyler and the MALLBRATS trash the park in a streetlight-illuminated, triumphant frenzy of vandalism and littering. Tyler leaves a note pinned to a fallen statue. The note reads: *I made this mess, and it felt great. I'm bonkers and my grime-fighting days are over. The hell with everything. Sincerely, The Bagman.*

INT. NEWSPAPER PRESS – DAY

The Burghers' Bugle rolls off the press. Headline: "Bagman flips out, trashes park, disappears."

INT. SANITARIUM – NIGHT

Bagman, now sporting a squalid straightjacket, is dumped by unseen forces into a padded cell. The door slams shut and a key turns into a creaky lock. The day's *Bugle* is placed carefully near his motionless face.

INT. BART'S KITCHEN – DAY

Twist-Tie Kid sits at the table, staring at the candle and the amulets, nervously tapping both feet.

TWIST-TIE KID

Where can he be? (beat) I hope that his situation isn't hazardous, Lazarus. (beat)

The least he could do is set off his heat-activated distress signal if he's up the creek.

INT. HEARING OFFICE – DAY

One of the three orderlies pushes Bagman in a wheelchair, still costumed, straightjacketed and heavily sedated, before a panel consisting of the CHAIR and two other BOARD MEMBERS. Lucius and Laverne sit amid piles of incriminating files.

CHAIR

Barton P. Backus, by the authority vested in this panel, I advise you that a prima facie case of mental incompetence has been made, and that this hearing will determine the issue.

The Chairman glances at fellow panel members, who nod back in unison.

CHAIR (CONT'D)

Mr. Backus, you have the right to be represented in these proceedings. Have you had the opportunity to retain and instruct counsel?

Tyler bursts hurriedly into the room, carrying an expensive (and obviously stolen) briefcase.

TYLER

He sure has, you chairship. Me.

CHAIR

Aren't you a little young for this, Mister—

TYLER

Uh, Mason. And don't hand me that "young" guff. The law doesn't stop anyone from representing the nut cases—uh, subjects—of these proceedings.

Bagman regains consciousness, groans loudly and falls back into a stupor.

CHAIR

Mr. Mason, your client does not look well.

TYLER

I guess that's why we're here, huh?

CHAIR

Mr. Mason, I am ordering an adjournment until tomorrow morning. At that time, I expect to see Mr. Backus more than five per cent conscious. Do I make myself clear?

TYLER

Yeah, sure.

INT. HEARING OFFICE CORRIDOR – DAY

As an orderly wheels Bagman down the hall, our hero stirs. A cafeteria comes into view.

BAGMAN

Beans! Beans!

ORDERLY
What did you say?

BAGMAN
I've got to have beans. I'm on a special protein diet. To ward of toxic urban pollutants.

The orderly stares at him in amazement.

BAGMAN (CONT'D)
My specialist says I need to eat beans at least once a day. I haven't eaten. I've got to have beans!

ORDERLY
Are you out of your mind?

BAGMAN
Not this again. Look, just swing by the cafeteria. It's not disorderly conduct to let a guy eat.

ORDERLY
Two minutes. Or they'll have my arse.

The orderly shakes his head and stops at the cafeteria.

INT. CAFETERIA – DAY

ORDERLY
You're in luck, pal. Today's special is yesterday's beans. But you're stayin' in the jacket and chair.

INT. CAFETERIA – DAY (LATER)

Bagman devours the fare, spoon-fed by the orderly. After a few moments, Bagman glances back at his butt and smiles.

INT. BART'S KITCHEN – DAY

Twist-Tie Kid's candlelit vigil is interrupted by the ringing of The Bagman's heat-activated sensor.

TWIST-TIE KID
Ha! He got to the beans again, Ben.

Gripping his homing device, Twist-Tie Kid darts to a closet and emerges, disguised as an old lady.

INT. SANITARIUM VISITING ROOM – DAY

A disguised Twist-Tie Kid sits at a table opposite Bagman, who is groggy and free of his straightjacket, but unwashed. Both Twist-Tie Kid and the orderly by the door hold their noses and fan their hands towards Bagman, who reeks royally.

BAGMAN
Nice getup, kid. Could have belonged to my grandmother.

JASON
Um, it did belong to your granny, Manny.

BAGMAN
Oh. (beat) So what do you want?

JASON
What do I want? To get you out of this hole, Noel.

BAGMAN

Why bother, kid. The jig is up. The MALLBRATS are running wild, the city's a mess, and everyone thinks I'm several cans short of a blue box.

JASON

Come on, Juan. You told me that it ain't over 'til the last garbage truck rolls out. (beat) Besides, think of our parents, Clarence.

BAGMAN

Mom. Dad.

JASON

And think of all the kids who look up to you, Lou. Burgherville needs The Bagman. Who else is going to stop the MALLBRATS? And as of this morning, we've got a hot lead, Reid.

BAGMAN

Kid, I'm not any more crazy than the next guy.

In the background, an obviously deranged MENTAL PATIENT stumbles around the room, repeatedly trying to sit on an imaginary chair, and failing.

BAGMAN (CONT'D)

I've got to get out of here, and bag Pritzlaff. Without him, they're toast.

Jason hands Bagman a nicely folded pile of clothes.

JASON

Take these duds, Bud. The staff here were happy that your old granny was bringing them. So happy, in fact, that they never noticed the orderly's gown hidden in the pile, Lyle.

BAGMAN

Kid, in the garbage bin of life, you're a true deodorizer. I can just change and walk right out of here!

JASON

We can't chance your failing to clear the security decks, Rex. But you could take the garbage chute. It's a two-storey drop, but the bin's half-full, so you won't get hurt, Bert.

BAGMAN

I can see this isn't going to be a great week for personal hygiene.

INT. SANITARIUM CORRIDOR – DAY

Bart, now wearing an orderly's uniform and carrying his costume in a sealed bag, slips out of his room. He opens a nearby door marked *Garbage Room,* looks left and right, enters the room and closes the door behind him.

INT. BART'S DINING ROOM – DAY

Bart and Jason sit around the table with candle and amulets.

JASON

So we can nail the MALLBRATS once and for all, Paul. One of my pals hides out in garbage bins outside the hot teen spots, working undercover for Sanitation. He got a hot tip on their favourite hangout as a rule, Abdul.

BART

So you heard it through the crapvine.

JASON

Right. They meet at happy hour at the Zowie-Blam Arcade, at West Jen-Erik Shopping Centre, Spencer.

BART

The mother of all malls.

Bart pounds the table with such force that his framed portrait of Rachel Carson now hangs crookedly on the wall.

BART (CONT'D)

Kid, I have a plan. Load up the Bagmobile with about half a tonne of garbage before happy hour at the Zowie-Blam Arcade.

JASON

Will that be fresh garbage or rotten garbage?

BART

Fresh.

JASON
Perishable or non-perishable?

BART
Perishable.

JASON
Double or single bags?

BART
Double. It could get rough in there.

Bart and Jason stand up and direct their attention to the candle and amulets.

BART/JASON
We vow to bring garbage to justice. And to always segregate the recyclable stuff.

EXT. MALL – NIGHT

Bagman and Twist-Tie Kid enter the mall. They haul many heavy bags of garbage.

INT. MALL—ARCADE EXTERIOR – NIGHT

They painstakingly erect a bag-barrier around the arcade, much to the bewilderment of onlooking SHOPPERS.

BAGMAN
The Baginot Line is up.

TWIST-TIE KID
Let's rock and roll, Cole.

The Bagman produces a megaphone.

BAGMAN
(through megaphone)
Tyler Pritzlaff and all you MALLBRATS in there, this is a raid!

INT. ARCADE – NIGHT

Tyler looks up in alarm from his video game, a battle between futuristic garbagemen and renegade litter-fiends called *Trash of the titans.*

BAGMAN (O.S.) (CONT'D)
Come out with your tokens up!

TYLER
All of you take out Twist-Tie Kid. Meet back at the hole at nine.

INT. MALL – ARCADE EXTERIOR – NIGHT

Tyler bolts out of the arcade. Turning over a garbage can, he climbs to the top and jumps over the Baginot Line. Tyler's team of transgressors emerges and overpowers Twist-Tie Kid. They muss his hair and blow cigarette smoke in his face.

TYLER
(to Bagman)
You'll have to catch me first, Bag breath!

A dramatic chase ensues, during which a skateboarding Tyler leads Bagman through the mall. Tyler punctuates his flight by knocking over garbage cans, storefront displays and a popcorn stand, leaving a horrendous trail of litter and confused shoppers in his wake.

Following Bagman are the butterfly net-toting Lucius and Laverne, the three orderlies from Sigmund's Semi-Private Sanitarium and two of MacDreck's OFFICERS.

At length, Bagman realizes he's being followed and grinds to a halt. He looks at the fleeing Tyler ahead of him and the huffing gang following him.

BAGMAN
(to himself)
If I take the side exit, I can get away to fight again another day. On the other hand, if I bag Pritzlaff, the city will be clean again. But by the time I do, that motley crew will probably bag me.
(beat) Only one choice here.

Bagman dashes off in pursuit of Tyler.

EXT. PARKING LOT – NIGHT

Bagman doggedly tails Tyler to the bus terminal, where a bus gears up to pull out. Tyler, far ahead on a skateboard, turns to shout a parting taunt.

TYLER
You're finished, Bags! They won't let you out 'til you're too old to remember why they put you away!

Tyler drops a gum wrapper and gives Bagman the raspberry.

TYLER (CONT'D)
So long, Mr. Clean!

In taking his eyes off the pavement, Tyler does not see an apparently discarded pop can in his path. His skateboard trips over the can, sending him hurtling through the air, hands and feet flailing, and careening into a gargantuan garbage can.

Tyler lies on the pavement, dazed, his fallen earring landing beside him. Bagman binds Tyler's hands and feet with garbage bags, then picks up the can and the earring. He drops the earring on the half-dazed Tyler's stomach.

BAGMAN
I believe you dropped this.

TYLER
You freak. If it wasn't for that damn can.

BAGMAN
Funny, isn't it?

Bagman smiles at the can in his hand. It bears his own tree logo. He tosses it over his shoulder into a recycling receptacle next to the garbage can.

BAGMAN (CONT'D)
When it comes to cleaning up this town,
maybe baggers *can* be choosers.

The three orderlies, the two officers and Lucius and Laverne arrive, followed by MacDreck.

LUCIUS
(indicating Bagman)
That's him! That's him!

The officers handcuff Bagman. MacDreck checks on Tyler.

INT. HEARING OFFICE – DAY

Back at Bart's competency hearing are the panel, a BAILIFF, Lucius and Laverne, Twist-Tie Kid, MacDreck, a MOB of well-wishers, and a flurry of PHOTOGRAPHERS and REPORTERS. The mob includes the survivors of Tyler's earlier assault with the billboard, carrying the signs from that fateful protest march, and wearing necklaces bearing replicas of Brett and Blanche's tree-shaped amulets.

CHAIR
We have heard the evidence this morning. Evidence including newspaper reports, affidavits and photographs submitted by the neighbours, Mr. and Mrs. Lavang...

Lucius raises his arm in triumph, while Laverne scans a luxury travel brochure.

CHAIR (CONT'D)
... one rock video, and your own behaviour, which is eccentric at best, psychotic at worst. We find ample evidence to suggest that your mental competence is far from certain.

The room erupts into a crescendo of boos and hisses in support of Bart.

MOB
Have a heart! Give us Bart! Don't be a drag! Undo The Bag!

BAILIFF

Order! Order!

CHAIR

However, we also find that you have not harmed anyone, broken any rule or committed any crime. (beat) Sartorial considerations excepted, of course.

Some murmured, offended jeers erupt from the mob.

CHAIR (CONT'D)

And we are satisfied from Mr. Pritzlaff's self-incriminating statements to Commissioner MacDreck that you are not responsible for the park incident. Thus, we conclude that you, Barton P. Backus, also known as The Bagman, are free to go.

The crowd cheers wildly. A beaming Jason shakes hands with MacDreck and members of the audience. Lucius and Laverne cry on each other's shoulders. Reporters and photographers scrum The Bagman.

MOB

Plant trees, not trash! Bring back clean air! Don't be a chump, can the new dump!

CHAIR

(over the din)

And we direct Mr. Backus in his capacity as The Bagman to keep up the good work, and to get a tetanus shot to avoid possible infections.

EXT. BART'S STREET – DAY

As a smiling and whistling Bart passes the Lavang house, he sees the two Sanitation officers haul Lucius and Laverne away in a pedal-powered paddy wagon. Bart waves at them cheerfully. They don't seem to notice.

A few steps later, he sees Tyler and the rest of the MALL-BRATS in crisp, white Sanitation uniforms. They are supervised from a comfortable, shady spot by their new probation officer—Jason—as they sweep curbs, pry bubble gum off the sidewalk and collect unscooped dog poop.

FADE OUT.

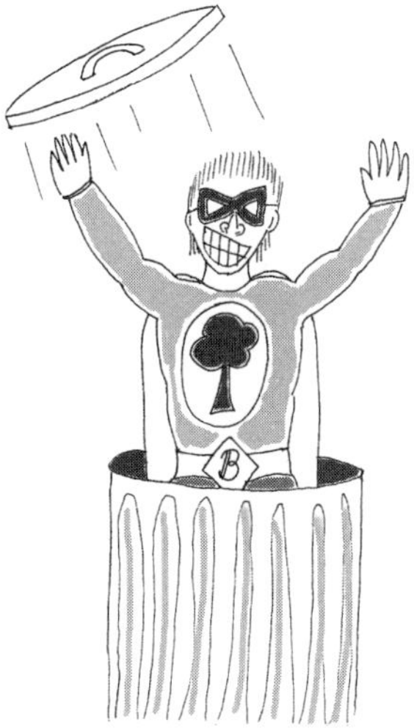

Rules for keeping the planet green

Source
Patti-Jo Robichaud

Occupation
Semi-pro hockey player

Residence
Buctouche, New Brunswick

Motto
"Frankly, Scarlett, I don't give a puck."

Rules

1 Poke-check litterbugs into submission.

2 Pretend tossed pop cans are pucks, and trash cans are nets.

3 Reduce the demand for landfill space by compacting garbage with a Zamboni.

4 Save energy by easing off on cannonading Sunday drives, spinerama dryer cycles, and of course, peak-hour power plays.

5 Punish industrial polluters by slashing their government bailouts, high-sticking them with hefty fines, and hooking them up with a probation officer who'd make Eddie Shore look like Lady Byng.

6 Cut down on noxious CO^2 emissions big-time by muzzling hyper announcers, colour commentators and fans.

Millennium madness

53

A fond look back at looking forward

WHEN HISTORIANS DO A POST-MORTEM on the final years of the 20th century, they'll find a surreal sense of urgency. Sort of like the wind picking up before the big tornado scene in *The Wizard of Oz,* but with the part of the Wicked Witch played by a calendar, and her evil cackling replaced by the countdown of seconds on a clock.

Psychologists have even come up with the term "Millennium Anxiety"—not for an emerging medical condition, but a new business opportunity.

There's an enormous sense of imminence, even foreboding, out there. And I'm not ready. I know I'm supposed to be doing something, but I haven't the slightest idea what. I'm sure there must be some rules out there. So I do what any law-minded slob does: when in doubt, check how people screwed it up in the past. That way, the mistakes I make will be fresh and original.

Wouldn't you know it, there are precedents on point.

At the end of the 19th century, the salons of Europe burst with a cathartic movement in art, literature and music called *fin de siècle.* It was a time of new ideas (anarchy was a popular subject, but no one could agree on the rules), new technology (motor vehicles, motion pictures, motion sickness) and the avant garde (which would eventually dwindle to garde). The faithful believed that the appearance of a couple of zeros at the end of the year was a signal to fix every wheel on earth, especially those that weren't broken. Imagine hundreds of Victorian Tom Peters clones on opium, and you begin to get the picture.

It was even worse when the first millennium turned. Most folk couldn't give a gutted goat's head about calendar-watching, being preoccupied with avoiding starvation, disease and pattern baldness. But devout Christians armed with Revelation 22 swore that at 12:01 a.m. on January 1, 1000, Gabriel's horn would blow and the kingdom of heaven would open for business. When the golden hour arrived and the Almighty failed to show, they pretty much shut up and went back to copying out scriptures and praying for someone to invent the photocopier.

Fast-forward to a world where yesterday's miracle technology is today's antique, and watch the anxiety multiply. It's nuts.

Governments and the media urge us to get busy planning our celebrations. People made party arrangements years in advance—a truly repulsive concept to those of us who won't stop, look or listen at uncontrolled intersections because it would spoil the spontaneity of the experience.

My cousin tried getting on one of those millennium cruises by luxury liner to the Holy Land over New Year's in 1999. Booked solid. The closest thing he could get was riding shotgun for a cod-poaching operation off the coast of Labrador—in the year 2999.

Everywhere you look, you see well-meaning folks clamouring for new hope and renewal for humanity—a millennial call for peace, environmental sustainability and an end to hunger. That's a pretty tall order. All I want for the new millennium is a sugar substitute that tastes good, but won't make you choose between surgery and radiation.

There are thousands of millennial happenings underway already. Sure, there are the usual marathons, quilts and civic projects. What's missing are more creative galas, like *Awakening 2000,* a global, satellite-linked, round-the-clock celebration of insomnia. How about *Apocalypso 2000,* a hip-swaying, bongo-bashing dance party for the rhythmic doomsday crowd? Or even *Booger 2000,* an ambitious plan to encircle the nations of the world in a festive, humongous ribbon of mucus.

The high watermark of Millennium Anxiety is the so-called Year 2000 problem, the latest from a vast and ancient sea of doomsday scenarios. Reports say that the paddlewheels of civilization will grind to a halt, and organizations will spend $300-$600 billion to fix this holy terror. Wouldn't it be cheaper to just pull the plug and go back to the Stone Age? Even a few lousy hundred million would buy ample venison, fur and cave space to go around.

You talk about doomsday, and most people get terrified. But sometimes, the total annihilation of the universe doesn't seem so bad. If you've ever spent an evening vetting financial statements at a volunteer board meeting, digging out bellybutton lint or playing right field, you'll know what I mean.

It's only a matter of time until all of this doomsday stuff goes mainstream.

Our politicians will be quick to respond to the apocalypse.

The Reform Party will say that it's all Central Canada's fault.

The Prime Minister, a puddle of calm in a sea of panic, will tell us to relax, and assure us that the end of the world will soon pass, and everything will go back to normal.

The federal Progressive Conservative Party will claim that it's the best equipped to lead us into eternity, since as far as it's concerned, the world already ended with Kim Campbell.

Not to be outdone, the Parti Quebecois will insist on Quebec's inalienable right to blow up *separately* from the rest of Canada.

Naturally, the media will get into the act as well. Can't you just see the headlines:

- *The Globe and Mail:* Toronto municipal amalgamation threatened by nuclear meltdown
- *Canadian Living:* 99 handy decorating hints for Judgment Day
- *Reader's Digest:* Don't let the coming holocaust get you down: one brave woman's story
- *Sports Illustrated (Leadsuit edition):* Are your next year's season's tickets refundable?
- *The National Enquirer:* "Elvis pressed the button from beyond!"–Former White House official
- *Saturday Night:* Why the Almighty is bitchin' mad, and not gonna take it any more: the exclusive interview.

And of course, the CBC: "This just in. The world will end at 9:00 o'clock tomorrow morning. Meanwhile, millions of Canadians are stampeding to Newfoundland, where the world is not expected to end until 9:30."

Okay. Let's assume that the world will not expire at the millennial moment. What do we do? Well, it's still a swell excuse to get our act together. My friend Zack finally came to grips with his split personality. He told his boss that he hadn't been himselves lately, and he needed time off to get some professional help. It worked out pretty well. They only downsized one of him.

Another millennium project: you could completely renovate your home. The Maharishi's minions have a master plan for all the bungalow owners in the cosmos to build special high-ceilinged studios for yogic flying. Unfortunately, they're having trouble getting it off the ground.

How about putting together a family history? You'll be astonished, even delighted, at what you might find. Take my great-grandfather, Miklos Takach. He wasn't the brightest guy in his village. In fact, he made it to Village Idiot, and after many years of intensive practice and lobbying, to District Idiot. Eventually, in a gruelling competition, he earned the coveted title of County Idiot. But he never achieved his lifelong dream: to be Grand National Idiot of the Austro-Hungarian Empire. Too much competition from those damned yodellers.

A really fun thing about the millennium: the baby boomers will blossom into senior bloomers. After besieging us with the "S & Ms"—everything from surfing tunes and sit-ins to marathons and mutual funds—they will boldy move on to give us the geriatric version of the 4-H club: home care, hip replacements, hemorrhoids and the hereafter.

Can't you picture it? Ads will use less and less cute babies, and more and more cute elderly people:

MAN

After putting up with dad's old, hand-me-down couch for years, Peg and I finally got this lovely new one. So when Dad comes to visit, we want to make sure *it's* protected.

DAD

That's right, son. That's why we use *Mr. Incontinent*—the new, comfortable, fold-lock, thermo-zip, industrial-strength protection that won't spring a leak whenever *I* take one.

Our attitudes will change tremendously. By the time the ad biz gets done with Alzheimer's, it won't be a dehabilitating disease. It will be a convenient and cost-effective way to forget about everything else that's ailing you.

But the biggest pain of all about this whole millennium thing is that nobody knows exactly when it will happen!

Most people assume the new millennium will start at the end of 1999. But the lab coat crowd says it won't occur until December 31, 2000, at precisely 12:00 midnight (12:30 in Newfoundland).

Another bunch of guys with tweed jackets, bifocals and scraggly little beards tell us that the whole Year 2000 business is a fraud. They say that when we started keeping the AD calendar back in the year 532, the monk responsible—the aptly named Edward the Short—bungled the math. On top of that, there's new evidence that Jesus was actually born in about 5 BC.

So the bottom line is, don't worry about what to do, or how to behave, around the turn of the new millennium.

Thanks to a mathematically challenged monk who's been worm food for almost 1500 years, when the millennium actually did turn back in the mid-1990s, you probably spent the magic, once-in-a-lifetime moment flossing, lip-synching to a *Seinfeld* rerun or scraping cat puke off your rug.

Rules for coping with change

Source
Aloysius "Big Al" Makamuna

Occupation
Palm leaf hatter

Residence
Somosomo, Fiji

Motto
"Surf's up."

Rules

1 Beware of the first stage of change: denial. The feluccas are nice, but the beaches are fraught with crocks.

2 If you build your castle on the shoreline before high tide, be prepared for a sunken living room, lots of water closets and wall-to-wall wet bars.

3 When a shark bites into your boogie-board, learn to let it go. And be darned quick about it, too.

4 If your beach party merges with another and you find your blanket squeezed out, become an agent of change. Come back at night with a metal detector and scoop their lost coins. Feel free to take their rings and Rollexes, too.

5 When your cherished spot under the palm is taken, take time to grieve. *Then* fire up the chainsaw.

6 If all else fails, break out a ukulele and belt out chestnuts from the motivational speaking industry, like *Brother, Can You Paradigm?*

Coming soon, to a theatre of life near you

55

Where we're headed, and the rules that will follow us there

When asked what the fates held in store for the world, the great 20th-century philosopher, Lawrence Peter Berra, better known to an adoring public as Yogi, declared that "The future ain't what it used it be." When the inevitable battery of sociologists, psychologists and futurologists dissected that edict, they concluded that there was profound merit beneath its deceptive simplicity, and that the New York Yankees' Ugly Duckling was not as big a quack as they had thought.

Central to Mr. Berra's bold thesis is the notion that the future, like Whitey Ford's fastball on a good day, is a moving target; that our concept of the future is evolving as much as we are.

Over the ages, predicting the future has enjoyed a vogue rivalled only by favoured pastimes like stoning, fighting the Black Plague, and pari-mutuel betting. Almost 500 years ago, Nostradamus warned of the rise of the Third Reich, atomic warfare and the AIDS epidemic. On the other hand, as recently as 1977, a chap named Ken Olson told delegates at a convention of the World Future Society that "There is no reason for any individual to have a computer in their home."

In *It's a Matter of Survival,* Anita Gordon and David Suzuki describe the future as a hypothetical extension of the present. They reason, as did Yogi Berra before them, that understanding the needs of the present is essential to planning for our future.

With all of this in mind, let's look at our laundry list of pressing issues in the new millennium, and evoke the spirit of Nostradamus—if not Ken Olson—to project their evolution, and the inevitable legal fallout.

My way or the I-way

As we delegate an ever-increasing portion of our personal and working lives to the almighty semiconductor chip, we can foresee a world that is profoundly different than it is today. Since Mr. Olson's fearless prediction, the wave of information and communication technology has developed so fast that even the media clichés can barely keep up. The Internet balloons by thousands of users each time nature calls. Unfortunately, the analogy doesn't end there.

The Net—now there's a boffo opportunity to bring out the best in the brave new world. Case in point: did you know that you can file your taxes electronically? Simply dial into Revenue Canada; stick an intravenous needle and tube into your arm; hook the tube up to your modem; and drain your blood to them directly.

You can get great evening companions, too. My buddy signed up with one of those high-end, on-line computer dating services. They hooked him up with this stunning, very well-built, highly intelligent and rather fast laptop model.

Businesses finally discovered the Net as a means of reaching out and touching customers. For example, you can now contact the Mafia's main Web site in Sicily. They'll link up with a regional office close to you, and have one of their professional Human Resource Liquidators waste your pain-in-the-ass neighbour within 24 hours (excluding time off for mass), or you get the next hit absolutely free!

More and more services will appear on-line. Already, education competes with shopping and entertainment at your friendly home computer terminal. The implications are far-reaching. Video gym classes, with students doing synchronized finger push-ups. New health modules on pale skin, rhino rumps and carpal tunnel syndrome. A fresh bag of excuses for late assignments. ("Uh, my URL got unbundled and cross-hardwired with my hypertext DTH protocols, man.")

Will it be long before Microsoft buys the planet's public school systems, trades in all the desks for home computers and teaches our kids the stuff that really matters? "For an interactive learning session on our intrusive, bureaucratic and evil monopoly laws, click on Dale the Doodlebug…"

How about health? "Thank you for calling Cyber-Doc™. For life-threatening situations, please click on the detonating bomb icon, and take a few moments to review the end-user agreement and disclaimer. If you require software to unzip this document, we have links to several competitively priced providers…"

The administration of justice will move to cyberspace as well. Imagine filing court documents by e-mail. "If this affidavit moves you like it did me, please send it as an attachment to 300 of your closest personal friends."

Or appearing before a judge through computer video-conferencing. "Excuse me, Your Honour, but is my monitor screwed up, or have you been getting like *way* too much sun?"

Think of virtual reality prison cells for convicts. "Guilty as charged. You are hereby sentenced to 20 years on Gilligan's Island, with no eligibility for rescue for 15 years."

As much as society as a whole will benefit from these miracles, the real winners in the I-way sweepstakes will be hackers and lawyers. What attic anarchist worth his weight in zit strips could resist the opportunity to destroy the justice system? And what self-respecting bar-type wouldn't salivate at the looming mountain of lawsuits for cyber-glitches that cyber-crap on people's property and dignity?

Already, your local constabulary is busy photographing speeding cars and mailing tickets to their puzzled owners. Will it be that long before their cameras move to street-front lampposts and focus on more serious offences, like loitering and squeegie-scrubbing? They could broadcast the action live on the Internet, and then hire and wire shut-ins to monitor the proceedings, and e-mail the nearest cop shop when bad things happen.

Global and mobile

In the brave new world of international business and instantaneous communication, people will telecommute to work in different countries and continents every day. They'll take part in global town hall meetings as easily as they change their underwear—though hopefully not at the same time. Just picture it:

ANNOUNCER

Nigel lives in New Sarepta. He works in Kuala Lumpur. His alimony cheques go to Bashaw, Wawa, Sagenaw, Moosejaw, and St-Louis-de-Ha-Ha. He gets his lunch from the Sandwich Islands, his hair gel from Greece, and his designer drawers pressed in a former Iron Curtain country. His proctologist practises in Tsushima. So once a year, he Fed-Exes his ass to Japan!

With people, products and commerce flowing across borders and oceans like grounders dribbling through Bill Buckner's legs, nationality and citizenship will blur into a mammoth maze.

Governments will continue to give way to global, entrepreneurial organizations promising better public services and greater efficiency, without the inconvenience of elections.

Everyone's favourite Satan, the banks, will merge into multinational conglomerates; hike their service charges to the stratosphere; and double their customer service representatives from one to two. Capital, labour and technology will dance the transnational tango, proving that the best diplomats are readily convertible currencies.

All of this will throw traditional, local legal systems into a frenzy of information-gathering, harmonizing and outright panicking. It will get even tougher to find out whose laws rule.

For example, how on earth would the law handle a claim by a punk from Pittsburgh, punctured by a defective coin-operated body-piercing machine at a skinhead theme park in Linz, where the machine runs software produced in Peoria under licence from the manufacturer in Manila, and is leased through a Burmese broker from its owner, a Kenyan conglomerate, which financed it at a Japanese bank, mortgaged it to a creditor in Wagga-Wagga, and had it fabricated in a Finnish factory? Only law school exams used to be like this. (The correct answer, by the way, is to bludgeon the punk and forget the whole sorry mess.)

Creeping chronographs, Batman

We have all heard and read the demographic projections. Canadian birth rates are decreasing, and our life expectancies are increasing. One doesn't have to be a thinker of Yogi Berra's calibre to divine that this translates into a glut of elderly folks, particularly when the baby boomers start reverting to diapers around the year 2025.

Again, the legal ramifications will be vast, as Canadians seeking to retire sue the federal government—or whatever will be left of it—for their unrefunded contributions to the Canada Pension Plan—whatever will be left of *it*. Everyone will have to make their facilities more accessible to those nifty little power-carts, at the risk of violating the coming litany of seniors' rights legislation. Cosmetic surgeons and pharmaceutical patent lawyers will buy beachfront properties on the Spanish Riviera.

Natural law

Having spent eons wearing down the planet, we're under growing pressure to pay the eco-piper. Global warming and climatic change. Bad air days. Deforestation. Overpopulation. Toxic contamination. The mass extinction of species. It's enough to make you want to write a letter, get in your air-conditioned minivan, run over a deer, drive to the post office, stand in a long lineup and courier it somewhere.

Issues like landfills will become an even more fertile dumping ground for public consultations. The legal landscape will shift as we try to tame technology with a raft of rules for the new Three Rs: reduce, retread and rehash. The tobacco lobby will lead the ensuing industrial backlash on constitutional and all other grounds imaginable, but will ultimately go up in smoke.

On the hyper-natural front, advances in genetic manipulation will be slowed, but not stopped, by equal rights laws and lawsuits propagated by the emerging underclass of synthesized bio-mutants. Cloning jokes will be shelved—sheepishly.

And we'll keep coming up with great terms like "sustainable development" to make us all feel better.

Sound bite society

The age of diminishing attention spans has lopped the length of the average clip on the television news from almost 40 seconds to less than 10 in a single generation. Add a surging, synthesized rhythm track and we've got everything we need to keep from having to think in any detail at all. Even the last bastion of rational Canadian thought—the hockey arena—has been dumbed down to a cacophony of sirens, flashing lights and "official" T-shirts fired into the crowd at high velocity by slingshot.

This worries some people. But don't think of it as intellectual anarchy. Think of it as bringing attention deficit disorder to the masses.

Our era of instant self-gratification, brokered by those baby boomers, has seen special interest groups create a culture of victimhood that urinates on the very fire hydrant of society. Disgruntled souls thwarted in their quest for spiritual salvation will launch proceedings against the Almighty, in whatever form they choose to find Him, Her or It. Not every splintered faction will find a good home, but they will surely have a lobby. The insidious result is the political correctness movement—the verbal equivalent of another kind of movement altogether. (More on this on page 47.)

Naturally, the law will evolve to account for this.

Cumbersome statutes and contracts will be butchered and repackaged by the plain language police for easier consumption. Only they'll use point-form bullets instead of the traditional metal kind.

The future is wow

In these heady days of millennial mania, we should recall the words of the great Canadian literary critic, William Deacon. Well, maybe not all of them, because he said an awful lot of stuff. But he did liken entering a new century to passing through an open door. "Prophecy is futile," he wrote, "the possibilities are infinite."

Today, we find ourselves peering, wide-eyed, at a panoply of possibilities so formidable and far-reaching that predicting them with any semblance of accuracy seems as plausible as Yogi Berra catching a falling asteroid in a butterfly net.

But surely we can do more than count on futurology, Ouija boards or the I Ching to guide us. As the great Russian writer, Leo Tolstoy, said, "Ask not what the future holds in store, but what you can do to live the way you want to live." Actually, this is a paraphrase of a translation. A more accurate version, which draws on an old Russian proverb, is, "Seize today, because the secret police may seize you tomorrow."

This applies as much to our laws as it does to our lives, no matter how wired, globalized, polluted, old or sound-bitten we become.

As Yogi Berra himself said, "You've got to be careful if you don't know where you're going, because you might not get there." Or better yet, "When you arrive at a fork in the road, take it."

Rules for predicting the future

Source
Alicia "Cleanup" Kurys

Occupation
Baseball, and sometimes grade five

Residence
Kennebunkport, Maine, USA

Motto
"Save the last bats for me."

Rules

1 Throw your baseball cards down a steep flight of stairs. The players who make it all the way to the bottom will sign with teams in bigger markets next season.

2 If you wanna kill a hot streak (I mean, like, *totally*), touch a baseline on your way back to the bench. Take your ball cap off. And change your clothes every day. (I mean, you wanna *win,* or you wanna *smell* nice?)

3 Reread all the old ball stats, mags and books you can find. They say, like, history repeats itself.

4 If you've got a doubleheader planned for the weekend, expect rain, a ton of homework and the makeup piano lesson from hell.

5 Here's one from my dad. Have your teammates close their eyes and stand stone-still. Then start hitting pop flies. Whoever gets nailed first will have bad luck for a month. Or until they see straight again. Whatever.

6 Like, when all else fails, bring in the pros. Get Chinese takeout and check the fortune cookies.

Lawsey, lawsey, lawsey

57

So why have rules anyway?

IF YOU'RE ASKING YOURSELF THIS QUESTION, you're not the first. Back in the 17th century, the philosopher Thomas Hobbes (no Calvinist, he) wondered why folks submit to authority, even to obnoxious monarchs who repress them, tax the stuffing out of them and never invite them to the royal costume ball. He concluded that we obey laws because it beats the hell out of anarchy, looting and poor public hygiene.

In looking for the key to this puzzle, a later philosopher, John Locke, called the rule of law a "social compact" in which citizens agreed on things like the appropriate use of makeup, and reserved the right to overthrow whoever made up the government if it didn't come clean.

Adding the requisite Canadian content to the discourse, lawyer and poet F. R. Scott defined the purpose of law as turning passion to reason. This is why the great Cree chief, Poundmaker, spoke for so many at his trial after the Riel Rebellion in 1885, when he declared, "The law is a hard, queer thing. I do not understand it."

So we return to the question, why have rules? If you have parried through the preceding pages, you may have detected a few thrusts behind the laws being lampooned.

An obvious role of the law is to resolve conflicts, be they between individuals (*'Twas the eve of fishing season,* #41), or an individual and the state (*Singin' in the court,* #37).

Our earliest rules dealt with resolving disputes. An eye for an eye. A tooth for a tooth. A stiff fine and an even stiffer boot off the bench for judges who changed their verdicts.

Conflict is a basis of the human condition. Without obstacles to surmount, our lives are devoid of purpose, challenge and fulfillment. And meaning. Not to mention ulcers, high blood pressure and migraines. Lack of conflict makes for not only lousy drama, but bland living. Challenges are why it's worth getting out of bed every morning.

Life in cave-dwelling days revolved around a single, simple conflict: eat or be eaten. Or as we say in today's corporate cave-dwelling days, if you're not at the table, you're on the menu. How ironic to uncage the new millennium and find 19th-century Darwinism at a new apex.

A second apparent thrust of the law is to give people a measure of security in protecting the fruits of their labours, if not the vegetables. This covers laws protecting property, and particularly the ever-emerging field of "intellectual" property (*High tech gets hip,* #47). The idea here is to promote invention and commerce by granting a limited monopoly to the creator or inventor through devices like copyright, patents and insipid TV jingles.

Other laws or rules are concerned with things like formal procedure (*Rules for proper parliamentary debate,* #14), safety and hygiene (*Rules for keeping a clean coffee room,* #20), appropriate behaviour (*Rules for adopting a global currency,* #44), environmental protection (*Rules for keeping the planet green,* #52) and even personal discipline (*Rules for looking good and feeling fit,* #50).

But there's a strong, common thread running through these and other thrusts of the law. In one form or another, they all seek to preserve order. Naturally, what is order for one may be pure pandemonium for another. And that's what makes humanity such a fascinating experiment.

With all deference to our loveable dreamers, the anarchists, it would be quite the hodgepodge trying to function in a world modelled on such social aberrations as the Winnipeg General Strike, the Richard Riot or the Calgary Stampede. Imagine a city where the citizenry shuts down the infrastructure, takes up random looting and turns into *Hee-Haw.* Whatever the outcome, we can rest assured that it wouldn't be pretty.

Order is very important to Canadians. Give the Americans their life, liberty and pursuit of happiness. Let the French keep their liberty, equality and fraternity. We've got peace, order and good government! And darned if we didn't feel so strongly about it (now get this) that we put it in our constitution!

The rules of order are everywhere. They follow us from delivery wards, playgrounds and classrooms to wedding halls, coffee rooms and auxiliary hospitals. Even dying triggers a set of rules, starting with the burning question: cremation, burial or taxidermy?

So why have laws, then?

Without laws, we would have no expression of our shared values; no common playing field for our endeavours; nothing to break, reconstitute and use as a basis for moving forward. Of course, we wouldn't have parliamentarians, lawyers or photo radar, either. But if every yin didn't have its yang, the delicate balance would be upset, and we'd have sticky rice all over the floor.

All of us sneer at rules in their insidious gaggle of guises, from constitutions, codes and customs to statutes, signs and superstitions. But the naked truth is that they express who we really are as much as our finest art, literature or music.

Most rules are not soaring eagles, bearing our loftiest hopes, our broadest ambitions and our deepest fears.

They are more like worms. They inch along, an inextricable part of our everyday reality, surfacing everywhere from rain-soaked hopscotch squares and bird's nests to tackle boxes and graveyards.

This is why most laws are fundamentally mundane, and one reason why we view its purveyors with more than the occasional soupçon of eye-rolling. (Other reasons surface *in Pop goes the weasel,* #7, and *How law and words go together like tar and feathers,* #15.)

Perhaps the best thing that can be said for the laws in our lives is that they actually make us free. By drawing ever-changing lines in the shifting sands of our consciousness, a reasonable set of rules liberates us to comb our own shores, and parasail to the heights of our own ambition, conviction and sentence.

Here lies the ultimate paradox of the human condition, and its true majesty.

If we had absolute freedom, many of us would find ourselves listless and unfocused once the initial euphoria wore off. But given a set of strictures—be they rules, chains or any other challenge—we are forced to dig deep, and harness all of our imagination, passion and backbone to produce our richest results.

Maybe that's why we have all of these rules.

Law-de-da *indeed!*

Applause

Many thanks to:

- The seasoned visionaries at Peppercorn
- Our titanic team of illustrators, led by a trio of my favourite folks on earth, hailing from three cities and having survived a combined 67 years of my friendship—and mercifully still counting (special thanks to Youze and Jawn)
- "Canada's Master Gatherer," John Robert Colombo, for graciously sharing the hilarious side of Robertson Davies
- Sir and Ma'am, for fortitude beyond the call of duty
- Mom and Pop, for celebrating their richly deserved freedom in Algonquin Park all those years ago
- B, P and F, the three golden rules against whom I am overjoyed to measure all else.

eureka!